"Alan Young's account of his memorable partnership with a horse is like the show that put them together: engaging and enduring."

—Charlton Heston

"Alan Young demonstrates that it's possible to be a responsible citizen, a gentleman, and a very funny performer at the same time."

—Steve Allen

"I have always known Alan Young to be a totally enchanting performer, and now he has written a book that not only proves this but reveals him as an exemplary fellow. It is a charming, humorous, moving, and witty memoir which reminds us how lucky we are to have had him in our lives for so many years."

—Roddy McDowall

"*Mister Ed and Me* caught the essence of Hollywood of the 40s, and I loved reading it."

—Howard W. Koch

"*Mister Ed and Me*—Alan's delicious. So was the show. So's the book."

—Cindy Adams, *New York Post* syndicated columnist

"Alan Young is forever Young, as is his obvious love of 'Mister Ed' and his 'Mister Ed' years. What a delightful book. It rests lightly on the soul and conveys the charm of a man who is to me not only Wilbur but a joy to have worked with and gotten to know."

—Stefanie Powers

"A funny and delightful book about life on the set when your co-star is a horse."

—Sherwood Schwartz, writer/producer of *Gilligan's Island* and *The Brady Bunch*

Mister Ed and Me

"Simple basic black."

"Me with some awards they gave me.
Wilbur was thrilled. I had hoped for some carrots."

Mister Ed and Me

Alan Young
with Bill Burt

ST. MARTIN'S PRESS, NEW YORK

Photo Acknowledgments:
All photos reprinted courtesy of CBS, Inc., except as indicated below.
Photos on pages 32, 65, 70, 71, 78, 82, 88, 90, 106, 117, 128, 140, 142, 145, and 184 reprinted courtesy of the Alan Young Collection.
Photo on page 66 reprinted courtesy of M.G.M.
Photo on page 134 reprinted courtesy of Paramount Pictures.

Design by Jessica Shatan

Library of Congress Cataloging-in-Publication Data
Young, Alan
    Mister Ed and me   /   Alan Young with Bill Burt.
        p.   cm.
    "A Thomas Dunne book."
    ISBN 0-312-11852-X
    1. Mister Ed (Television program)   2. Young, Alan, 1919–
  I. Burt, Bill.   II. Title.
PN1992.77.M59Y68   1995
791.45'72—dc20
                                                        94-47921
                                                        CIP

First Edition
10 9 8 7 6 5 4 3 2 1

To Mary
with love and gratitude

CONTENTS

FOREWORD

This book is in memory of my dear buddy, Mister Ed.

Even though we seldom spoke off the set and never double-dated, we loved and respected each other's private lives.

I never inquired into his affairs, and he never stuck his nose into mine. "Which is difficult for a horse," he once said, "because most of my face is nose."

Oh, we had our differences, of course, of course. Once, when we went for our usual morning ride, he wanted to be on top for a change—but two three days of that, and he saw the folly of it all.

Ed was not a horse, he was an actor—even though he looked on that fact as a bit of a comedown. This was established conclusively when our Japanese sponsor, Mitsubishi, invited us to film in Japan for six weeks.

Our producers made inquiries and found that the Japanese immigration authorities demanded one month's quarantine for all animals brought into the country.

"But this isn't an animal," our producers argued. "This is Mister Ed—an actor." Whereupon the quarantine was cut to two weeks!

My admiration for Japanese logic, or their sense of humor, went up by ten notches. By international decree, Ed was proved to be an actor. But we all knew that.

I am also most grateful to my new Scots friend, Bill Burt. His judicious editing and smooth rewrites were invaluable to this first-time author,

Many thanks also to Mark Silverstein of CBS for his assistance in obtaining photographs.

Here's your book, Ed. Long may you rein.

ALAN YOUNG
Studio City, California
February 1994

PART 1

Straight from Wilbur's Mouth

1

Getting to the Post

The Birth of "Mister Ed"...

Getting the Team Together

L ooking back, I guess that very first show is still my all-time favorite. I'll never forget the opening lines of "Mister Ed." *There I was as Wilbur, with my back to that sweetheart of a horse, leaning over his stall, dreamily thinking aloud:*

> WILBUR: Ever since I was a little boy I always wanted a pony. Of course it's been a long time since I was a little boy.
> ED: It's bin a long time since I was a pony.

At the sound of the voice, WILBUR freezes. Then he slowly turns and looks at the horse. He turns away, shaking his head unbelievingly. Then WILBUR turns back to ED.

> WILBUR: Did you say that?

There's no immediate response, so he turns away again.

> ED: Did you say it?

"Our last picture. I can't keep my eyes off that pal of mine."

WILBUR rushes over to ED and takes his head in his hands.

WILBUR: Now, with me looking right at you, say something.
ED: What'll I say?
WILBUR: Anything!
ED: "How now, brown cow"?

From that day on, I began sharing my life with a horse. It's been that way for more than three decades now.

For five of those years, I was on his back many times. And I'm pleased to report that he's been on mine ever since. It's never bothered me because, apart from the fact that I still get paid for it, Ed and I were the greatest of pals.

The year "Mister Ed" was first conceived, I was riding high on television, doing my own solo act. And quite successfully, too, thank you very much. In fact, I turned down the opportunity to team up with Ed the first time around.

It was 1952, and I had just received two Emmy awards for "The Alan Young Show." However, writing and starring in a live weekly television show was a draining experience.

The only way to get off this constantly accelerating treadmill was to do my show on film. So I approached Arthur Lubin, a well-respected director of motion-picture comedies, and asked whether he would direct my show on film. His answer was quick and direct: "No."

Arthur had just sold his rights to his enormously successful *Francis, the Talking Mule* motion-picture comedies which starred the talented young Donald O'Connor. He was eager to translate the talking-horse concept to television, and he wanted me to quit my own show and be part of his team.

"A what?" I gasped when he told me that his new TV idea revolved around a talking horse.

When the concept was fully explained to me, I must confess I found the whole idea about a Mister Ed as exciting as a damp beach. Sharing starring credit with a horse bothered me, too. After all, I was a comedian. I worked alone. I had a hit show on my hands. And if I did decide to take on a partner, I'd prefer one who cleaned up after himself.

Eight years later, I ran into Arthur again. By that time I was ready to listen. Since we last spoke, I had wound up my own television series, made a couple of at-the-time-unsung movies, spent some time in the land of my birth, Merrie Olde England, and was existing on "guest spots"—a career move that keeps the wolf from the door, but no farther away than the sidewalk.

Upon my return from England, Hollywood wasn't exactly knocking down my door for my services. I was just another face in the legion of the unemployed.

"This is all going to change," I told my wife optimistically. "Wait until 'Tom' opens!" "Tom" was *Tom Thumb*, a picture I made in England for that brilliant producer-director of fantasy films, George Pal, and Metro-Goldwyn-Mayer.

Tom Thumb was released eventually—and my optimism soon faded. I had trouble even finding a theater which was screening it. I eventually tracked *Tom Thumb* down to a small theater in Van

Nuys. It had opened dismally, without fanfare or publicity. MGM had either no faith or no money. Perhaps a case of both.

At least my old buddy George Pal had faith in me. He rang me up. He wanted me to play Rod Taylor's closest friend in the film *The Time Machine,* based on the H. G. Wells classic.

"Same money as *Tom Thumb?*" I asked hopefully.

"I'm afraid not that much. But you can do whatever you want with the characters. You'll have fun."

Fun I could have at the beach. I needed money.

"It's only $1,500 a week," George explained, "but I think I could stretch the shooting schedule to three weeks. Besides, if the picture's a hit, it could really do things for you."

That's all a desperate performer needs to hear. So I went with it. For *Time Machine* I had to play three parts: Philby, his son, and his son at the age of eighty. I decided to play Philby as a Scot, which would set me apart from the other English character actors. I dyed my hair a deep red for the role.

George was right, I did have fun. But as far as doing anything for my career, the picture and I fell short.

Once more the studio—again MGM—had given him a bare-bones budget.

For *The Time Machine,* special-effects wizard George had to go to a party-costume, cut-rate emporium called Moskatells, where he bought cheap hair for the Morlocks, the beastlike futuristic tribe that lived underground. Then he shot the characters in subdued lighting so the stitching on the ratty wigs wouldn't show.

For the scene in which I played the eighty-year-old, I was made up at 7:00 A.M. and sent to the back-lot location. Before leaving, the makeup man handed me a cake of makeup and a bottle of spirit gum.

"They aren't supplying a location makeup man, so if the rubber on your face begins to peel, just glue it back on yourself," he instructed me.

My scenes weren't shot until 4:00 P.M., nine hours later! By then the sun had dried up my bald pate, and my rubber jowls were

"Before he met me, Wilbur (Alan) tried working with a lot of other stars. Here he is in *The Time Machine* with Rod Taylor."

peeling like a diseased bloodhound. I managed to paste myself together for the scene. But every now and again, I would feel a *sproing* as another piece of my character peeled off and bit the dust. No dramatic close-ups for me that day.

The Time Machine has become a respected cult film, popular on the late-night television circuit. But, like *Tom Thumb,* its original release was a well-kept secret. The picture had a mediocre run and no impact.

My disappointment over this movie was dispelled when Arthur Lubin came back in my life, wanting to talk about a horse.

I was delighted to hear that since we first spoke, Arthur had interested my old friend George Burns in the project, not as an actor, but as the producer. George's lifetime partner, Gracie Allen, had just retired and, rather than go on as a single, he decided to produce for television.

George bought into the Ed package and, with Arthur directing, produced a half-hour "Mister Ed" pilot. For some reason, it didn't sell. None of the three networks was the least bit interested. The project was in limbo.

Then, thanks to an introduction arranged by General Service Studios chief George Nasser, Burns and Lubin teamed up with talented director-producer Al Simon, who had just wrapped up his successful Robert Cummings series, *"Oh, That Bob!"*

Al was enthusiastic about the idea, but he felt changes were necessary. To begin with, the original horse used in the pilot was a pathetic-looking nag. If the public was going to be attracted to Ed, he should be a fine-looking animal. Also, the story didn't revolve around Ed. It followed the actions of a large, cumbersome cast of characters, none of whom were particularly appealing.

George Burns agreed with Al's critique. And, as he had put up all the money for the original pilot, he naturally wanted to recoup at least part of his investment, which appeared to be going nowhere.

The pilot was cut and edited into a tight fifteen-minute presentation highlighting the basic concept, which was presented to MCA, the show's sales agent. Since it had already tried unsuccessfully to sell it a year earlier, MCA wasn't terribly enthusiastic. But as George Burns was one of its top clients, MCA felt it was politically correct to give it another try.

MCA presented the revamped package to the highly respected D'Arcy Advertising Agency. As good fortune would have it, the first man to see it was one of their most astute account executives, Steve Mudge.

Steve loved it. "The minute I saw it, I knew that this show has got to make it," he told me later. "It couldn't fail."

He knew that it already had been pitched unsuccessfully to the three major television networks, and there was no chance they would consider it again. But Steve had other ideas.

One of his accounts was the Studebaker Corporation, a small but old and respected automobile company based in South Bend, In-

"Lou Derman, our writer, is showing Wilbur the 'cups and balls' trick. Wilbur still can't do it."

diana. It was currently and valiantly competing with the Big Three in Detroit, and management wanted a television show to introduce its new creation, the Avanti, a beautiful automobile, way ahead of its time.

Studebaker executives were persuaded that putting their innovative Avanti together with a successful television show could put them back in hot competition with the industry giants.

Steve knew that Studebaker's budget was small, so he shrewdly drew up a unique marketing plan to compensate for the lack of funds. After winning Studebaker support, Steve contacted George, Al, and Arthur and urged them to start assembling a "Mister Ed" cast and production team.

Before I entered the picture, the first item on their agenda was a new script, putting more emphasis on the close relationship between Ed and his owner. To achieve this, they made a very wise decision: they signed the talented Lou Derman as head writer.

Now they were looking for a lead actor. I was told later that

"I had to pretend I didn't like Carol. Gosh, that was hard!"

George Burns made the suggestion, "I think we should get Alan Young. He looks like the kind of a guy a horse would talk to." Hmm, I didn't know what to make of that at the time.

They ran the fifteen-minute film pilot for me. If I had previously had any doubts about the show they were gone now. I knew right away this was for me. It was clean family fare, and the fantasy inherent in the concept provided a marvelous opportunity for co-medic confusion, and general off-the-wall creativity. So I signed a contract to do the show.

But I needed a wife. Al had previously cast Connie Hines in a pilot which hadn't sold. But she had come across so well, they knew she was just what they were looking for. She was definitely my TV wife Carol—you couldn't find a sweeter and prettier face.

We had a show, a writer, and a star. But who would buy it? That's where whiz kid Steve Mudge's marketing genius kicked in.

In a unique arrangement, Steve proposed that the Studebaker Company join with its individual dealers across America to finance the production. His idea was that when the dealers sold a car, they would contribute $25 to the pot. Studebaker would match them dollar for dollar, so that every car sold meant $50 toward the show. Studebaker loved the idea, but would the dealers go for it? After all, they were independent and might have other ideas.

Al asked whether I would travel to selected sales meetings at which the new and improved pilot film would be screened. My job was to help convince dealers that we had a surefire winner.

I remember flying to Chicago for the first meeting with the can of film in my hot, excited hands. Traveling on the same plane were Robert Kennedy, Sargent Shriver, and other Democratic headliners. Flush with success, they were returning triumphant from the 1960 convention, at which John F. Kennedy had been nominated for president. I prayed that some of their success would float my way. And it did.

Steve Mudge met me in the Windy City and directed me to a cavernous hotel convention room, where the atmosphere was cool and the situation looked bleak. We were greeted by a hundred or so dour, stony-faced car dealers. They had just finished a bad sales year. Indeed their profit chart for the past five years looked like a downhill slalom course.

Undaunted, I made my pitch. I explained our new approach to the show and what future shows would be like. Then we ran the brief pilot. At the conclusion, Steve asked, "Well, how many of you would like to buy this show?"

To our delight, every hand went up. We were on a roll. This scenario was repeated in several major cities and, as I recall, there was not one dissenting vote.

Within a matter of weeks, each dealer returned to his hometown to purchase the best time-slot he could on his local station. Whether it was prearranged or not I'm unsure, but to my delight—with only two exceptions—they all purchased the same day and time slot. Amazingly, we now had a syndication outlet with more stations than we would have had on a regular network!

This strategy was exactly opposite from the way shows are generally sold. Normally, the network presentation comes first. Then, after a successful run of three years or more, the show is sold into syndication.

A television trade magazine called the "Mister Ed" deal "the freak sale of the year." "Mister Ed" had slipped into the homes of America by the back door.

Don't get the wrong impression. "Mister Ed" wasn't without teething troubles. In fact our first half-hour show was such a mess that Studebaker was on the verge of canceling its sweet deal with us.

Only today can the truth about that be told.

Director Arthur Lubin was out of the country when our first show had to be brought in, so another director was hired. He was—or used to be then—a distant relative of George Burns and was supposed to have a fair reputation as a comedy director.

I began to question his reputation when, in the opening shot that established Carol and Wilbur, he had our backs to the camera!

In fact, their faces weren't established properly until well into the scene, and then only in full-length shots. I had an uneasy feeling throughout that first three days of shooting. But since my own experience until then was in live television, I deferred to his reputation as a director.

My first impression was verified when George Burns, Al Simon, and the brass from the studio and agency sat in the screening room to preview the opening show.

As it progressed, my heart and stomach sank lower into my body which, in turn, sank lower in the seat. The pace was off, the scenes were labored, and the camera angles missed much of the comedy. There were no laughs in the screening room.

When the show ended, the lights went up. Everyone sat silent. George Burns was in the first row, with his back to us all. After a moment or two, he rose and turned to the assembly.

"On behalf of me and my . . . family, I want to apologize to you all," he said. "This was terrible."

Walking away from the theater, I hung back. Along with my

heart and stomach, my feet were now dragging. Mickey Rockford, one of MCA's top agents, who also handled George, joined me at the rear of what was turning out to be a funeral procession.

"Don't worry, Alan," he consoled me. "George won't let it remain this way."

"What can he do now?" I asked.

"I haven't the slightest idea," Mickey replied confidently.

By the time the show went on the air, George had worked his magic, with the help of Arthur Lubin, who was now back at the helm.

Various scenes had been edited judiciously. Scenes had been altered. Arthur directed us splendidly, and the result was a good opening show with excellent reviews.

Steve Mudge's brilliant maneuver to get us on the air became the talk of the industry. How effective was his strategy? Well, let's fast-forward to early 1962 to find out. "Mister Ed" hit the headlines that year while the Federal Communications Commission was investigating the value of TV rating services. The agency's hearings were televised.

At one point, a member of the FCC panel asked how the televised hearings were doing in the ratings. This is how the front page of the *New York Herald Tribune* of Wednesday, January 30, 1962, reported the exchange:

FCC VS. THE TALKING HORSE . . .

A talking horse and a cowboy have both outpulled the Federal Communications Commission as a television attraction.

Interrupting a discussion of program ratings yesterday, while NBC's research vice-president, Hugh M. Belville, Jr., was on the witness stand, Commissioner Robert E. Lee asked: "I wonder what kind of rating this hearing would get?"

Mr. Belville grinned, reached into his pocket, and came up with these figures from Arbitron:

"Is that monkey smoking a pipe or what? They sure are crazy people."

PROGRAM	NETWORK	RATING	SHARE OF AUDIENCE
Mister Ed	CBS	23.4	47 percent
Maverick	ABC	12.7	26 percent
FCC Hearing	NBC	8.2	17 percent

Enough said? But let's get back to those earlier days when we were still trying to get off the ground. And, most important, my introduction to the star of the series.

The Mister Ed Company—headed by producer George Burns, and associates Al Simon and Arthur Lubin—made another brilliant move when they hired Lester Hilton, one of Hollywood's best animal trainers, and commissioned him to seek out the best-looking palomino stallion in Hollywood. The horse was to be purchased outright—not rented, as was usually the case.

Within a week, Lester found our star. His name was Bamboo Harvester, and he cost $1,500. He was a magnificent-looking animal who had once belonged to the president of the California Palomino Society and he had started out in life as a parade or show horse.

Two days later, his name was officially changed to Mister Ed, and he was gelded—a procedure that happens to many of us when we enter show business.

I was instructed to report to Lester's "spread" in the San Fernando Valley to meet Ed and pose for publicity pictures.

Ed was being boarded at Lester's "ranch," where he was the trainer's sole responsibility. The spread consisted of a tiny one-bedroom house, two stables, and a small training ring. Lester was a bachelor, and his creature comforts were few. Horses were his whole life.

As a young man, Lester had studied and worked for the famous trick rider–comedian Will Rogers, and his horseflesh know-how was second to none. "The only thing I don't know about horses is how to bet on them," he once told me sadly.

Until then, his most famous motion-picture accomplishment was training the talking mule in all of Arthur Lubin's popular *Francis the Talking Mule* pictures for Universal Studios.

"Les Hilton, Wilbur, and me. Les only used that whip on Wilbur."

"Edna Skinner knit me some booties, so I gave her a quick smooch."

Next up to be introduced to Ed was Connie Hines, now signed to play my wife Carol. Today, whenever I am interviewed about the Ed show, two of the questions I am asked consistently are "How did they get the horse to talk?" and "Was Connie Hines really so pretty?"

I was sworn to secrecy on that first question, but I'll let you in on a little bit of that best-kept secret later on.

As to question number two: Connie was and still is a beauty. Being the wife on a television comedy series is a challenging job, especially when, your husband has a talking horse as his closest friend. But for five years Connie handled her puzzled, patient frustration with classic ability.

Edna Skinner had just finished her run in the TV series "Topper" and was cast as our next-door neighbor Kay Addison, whose wry comments and crazed shopping habits drove her husband Roger to distraction.

Roger was played by Larry Keating, one of radio and television's most versatile performers. In radio, he was Bob Hope's first announcer, and he debuted on TV playing Harry Morton, Burns and Allen's next-door neighbor.

One day, after I had spent hours shooting commercials for our sponsor and was packing for a hectic cross-country publicity trip to New York, Larry said, "Son, on your next series, try to get a part as a next-door neighbor. No responsibility. Work a day and a half a week and collect your check."

Larry was making light of his tremendous contribution to the success of our show. The takes and double takes of Larry's reactions to Ed are among the show's truly funny highlights. Doing a scene with Larry meant working with a master.

The final member of the cast to be selected was a crucial one—the voice of Mister Ed—a unique role that has caused much debate among trivia buffs over the years.

Casting Ed's voice was considered the most difficult chore, as casting calls are usually sent out for voice-over specialists. Recordings are made. Then come endless consultations, comparisons, tests, and more tests. But in this case Ed's voice turned out to be one of the easiest calls our producers had to make.

Ed's voice was found one afternoon when Al and Arthur were visiting Lester and Connie and I were busy shooting publicity pictures with Ed. Lester was painstakingly getting Ed to pose properly as Al and Arthur looked on. Suddenly a drawling Midwestern voice boomed out from the little ranch house. "Hey, Lester, where d'yuh keep the cawfee?"

Al's eyes popped. "That's him!" he gasped.

The voice belonged to Allan "Rocky" Lane. He had been acting in pictures since 1928 and had starred in a number of westerns. But at that particular stage late in his career, like many other actors, he had fallen on lean times, and his buddy Lester was letting him sleep on his couch. Al lost no time in cutting a deal with Rocky.

At first Rocky was dubious. He may have lost money, but he still had his pride. What would his friends think when they learned he had been reduced to doing the voice of a horse?

But the cash sounded okay, and he finally agreed to do it—if Al and Arthur promised not to reveal his name on the credits. They agreed to protect his identity—and his pride.

Rocky was in his late fifties when he started speaking on Ed's behalf, but he looked younger. He had been a handsome leading man in the Hollywood of the late 1930s, a cowboy star in the 1940s, and now, in 1960, the voice of a horse.

Now he had no screen credit, no dressing room, and no parking space. His often-morose attitude could be well understood—not appreciated, but understood.

On the first script "read-through," the cast sat at a huge table chatting and getting to know each other. Rocky just sat and stared at us. He had a marvelous opportunity to ingratiate himself with everybody, but he ignored it completely.

Finally Arthur Lubin rapped on the table for attention. Arthur loved being in charge, and he was very good at it. "Children," he always said, although Larry and Rocky were his age or older, "let's all listen to your director!"

He then introduced us all. We had met each other many times before, but Arthur was a stickler for protocol. When he got to my introduction, I couldn't believe it. "Alan," he beamed, "this show is going to make you a big star, and you'll be a very funny man."

I had won two Emmys just before this: one for best comedy show, the other for best actor. But Arthur can be excused; he was a motion-picture man who never even watched TV. His consuming interests were movies, travel, and the finer things of life. And he lived it to the full.

In any case, I was grateful for the job. I felt no urge to respond to Arthur's blissful ignorance of my television awards. Also, I was speechless.

Rocky Lane seemed to take the slight worse than I did. When the rehearsal was over, he came straight over to me and barked, "Why didn't you say something?"

"Huh?" I ad-libbed cleverly.

"You were funny long before this show," he snorted indignantly.

"I used to watch you all the time. You're as funny as George Burns. Why didn't you correct Arthur?"

"Maybe because I'm as smart as George Burns, too."

Rocky gave me a look and a grunt and walked away. I knew he could be reached and we'd get along. And we did. At times it wasn't easy, but we did.

Rocky was a considerate man in spite of himself. The first time I had to ride Ed was in a scene where I was supposed to gallop up to a jump. The horse would come to an abrupt stop, and I would sail on over the jump by myself.

Of course we had a stunt rider ready to do the actual fall. But the director still needed me to gallop up to the jump and come to a halt. Then he would cut and photograph the double.

We rehearsed for the shot and I—or, rather, Ed—galloped up to the jump. I was hanging onto the mane, the saddle horn, and bouncing all over the place. My horsemanship was atrocious. I hoped no one noticed. At least I didn't fall off.

But Rocky was watching me. As we were preparing for the actual take, he sidled up to me. "You haven't ridden long, have you?" he asked.

"Not long."

"How long?"

"For about twenty seconds. Just now."

He looked at me with an expression as close to kindness and concern as he could muster, then whispered gruffly, "If you keep your toes pointed down in the stirrup the way you're doing, you're gonna sail over the jump better than any stunt man. Only you're not gonna land so good. Keep your heels down, toes up, press down on the stirrup, pinch your knees, lean back, and relax."

We did the shot in one take. I stayed in the saddle and almost looked good. Afterward I could swear my mentor Rocky almost smiled at me. I know I smiled at him.

After the third year, I guess Rocky had stepped on about as many toes as the weather would bear. I was called into the studio and was told that unless I had strong objections, the producers were

As I've always said to George Burns, "George, if you keep smoking cigars, you won't live long."

going to replace Rocky as the voice of Mister Ed. I could not object with any conviction as, while he had not been deliberately mean, Rocky had irritated everyone certainly and consistently, including me.

For two or three days I read with every top voice in the business. We made recordings, and the producers and I sat listening for hours. They were all great actors and read dramatically and convincingly, but no one sounded like Ed.

We finally all had to admit that Rocky was Ed, and Ed was Rocky. Separating them would be a tragic, perhaps fatal mistake.

Whether Rocky learned of our auditions and intent I will never know, but the following season he was much more mellow and cooperative.

The fact that the month before our fourth season he bought a racehorse might have had something to do with Rocky's transformation. He loved the track. His favorite occupation was going to the early-morning workouts, watching the horses run, and talking with the trainers and jockeys.

"He bought a racehorse?" Les Hilton was disgusted. "The guy

has finally got some money in his pants, and he's bought a horse? With training costs, boarding charges, food, and vet bills, he'll go broke in a month and be living at my place again."

Les was wrong. Miraculously, Rocky's horse won the first time out! From the beginning, the little mare did beautifully. Rocky was on easy street. It also made things easier for us on the set. Whenever things became troublesome, I could immediately defuse the situation by asking, "Rock, how's the mare doing?"

He would beam like a proud father reporting on his precious offspring, and harmony prevailed. Maybe the solution is: When in trouble, get a horse!

"Mister Ed" turned out to be one of the best things that ever happened to Rocky Lane. After the show clicked, Rocky came to Al and said now he'd like to get his name on the show's closing cast credits.

Al pointed out patiently that the credit: "Mister Ed, played by himself" had proven so intriguing to younger viewers that many were convinced Ed really talked!

"So you see we can't change horses in the middle of a series," Al told Rocky. "Why not leave things the way they are, and instead we'll give you a raise?"

Rocky agreed and, as you may have noticed in reruns, the credit continues to read: "Mister Ed, played by himself."

Even with all these talented performers, a show doesn't stand a chance without good writing and plotting. This is where George Burns's inimitable editing and comedy sense gave us a tremendous edge.

Lou Derman headed the crack writing team, assisted ably by Norman Paul, Bill Davenport, and George Burns's brother Willy. Of course George attended most of the early writing and story-planning sessions—long, painstaking affairs held in George's office. In the second season, I sat in on these story sessions. Other writers who were to join us included Larry Rhine and Ben Starr.

Lou Derman was one of the most dedicated, workmanlike writers I've ever met. Asked to rewrite a page or a whole script, he never complained but got down to business immediately. This is not a common trait among writers.

Lou was also meticulous at keeping Ed's character clearly defined at all times. I remember one planning session when George threw in a very funny line for Mister Ed. Everyone nodded and howled except Lou. He looked at George, shaking his head solemnly. "No," he said. "Ed wouldn't say that."

George was dumbfounded. "What do you mean, 'Ed wouldn't say that'? He's a horse. He'll say what we tell him to say."

"It's not in his character," Lou persisted.

"What character? He's a horse!"

"Not exactly. He's Mister Ed."

George stared at Lou coldly as we all sat quietly. George is a fair and lovely man, but he's capable of being quite explosive at times. After a moment, he took a long drag on his cigar, exhaled the smoke meditatively, and said, "Lou's right. Ed wouldn't say that line. Give it to Wilbur."

Despite my early doubts, working with a horse turned out to be the joy of my life. I often refer to the Ed series as my "hay days." They were among the happiest of my life. I can never understand actors who walk off a series because "it's become stifling," or they want to stretch their abilities, or expand their talents.

Those actors are missing a unique opportunity. Playing the same role each week forces an actor to dig deep within himself and stretch his abilities to continually come up with a range of different reactions, subtle changes in approach to ever-changing situations, and maintain an infectious level of excitement and enthusiasm. It's a magnificent challenge.

Here's a useful piece of TV trivia. Few people are aware that "Mister Ed" did not begin in the mind of television writers. The stories first appeared as a series in *Liberty* magazine on November 18, 1937, and were titled "The Talking Horse" by Walter Brooks.

"This is how many people were riding on my back, and I loved them all."

In the short stories, Ed was a rough-talking, homely nag. But Al Simon insisted that people in his shows must have class, sets must be beautiful and, above all, horses must be handsome.

In the magazine stories, the couple were Wilbur and Carlotta Pope. Everyone agreed that Carlotta was too operatic, and Pope a little religious. So Wilbur and Carol Post were born.

Thanks to a fantastic team effort, everything seemed to slide effortlessly into place: the cast was set, the script completed, the horse was at the post.

We were off and running!

2

They're Off!

And I've Got a Hit on My Hands

Getting together the first day of a new television series is like attending a cocktail party full of strangers.

Everyone is sizing up everyone else. There is a strong element of suspicion. Knowing they are likely to be working together for a long time, many are already establishing parameters.

We were shooting at George Nasser's General Service Studios in Hollywood, a friendly little operation. It had been home to "Ozzie and Harriet," "Burns and Allen," "I Love Lucy," and "Perry Mason," so most of the stage and camera crews were familiar with each other.

But the actors were a different story. Makeup and wardrobe crews are particularly wary of their thespian colleagues because they have to work more closely with them, and actors' egos and phobias can be tough to handle.

They had no such problem with my friend Ed. As soon as Ed walked out to the set everyone knew who the real star was. He was cooperative, friendly, and totally without artistic temperament.

"Isn't he great?" became the catchword of the company. Thanks to the good vibes put out by our equine star, individual egos fell by the wayside.

Today's television shows are normally purchased by the networks in packages of three or four at a time, sometimes more. And if a new show doesn't deliver good ratings or show its potential to do so within a short time, it's dead in the water—sometimes after only one airing.

When we got going in the early 1960s, show segments were bought in thirteen-week packages and were generally allowed that length of time to prove themselves. Of course, costs were less then.

The original "Mister Ed" pilot cost $71,000, and when the series began, each show was brought in for $55,000. Recently I worked in a series where each half-hour episode cost a quarter of a million bucks!

George Burns insisted on staging the first thirteen shows himself—to ensure that everything possible was being done to get off to a good start, I suppose. Whatever the reasoning, it was a great privilege to watch him in action. He was keen, perceptive, and somewhat of a perfectionist. George is one of those professionals who knows exactly what he's after and goes after it determinedly.

George's hands-on involvement meant that the cast had to be prepared, which meant meeting each day before actual filming. With his marvelous ear for timing and delivery, George would direct us in our movements and sometimes in our line reading.

One day he turned to me and said, "Do you want to get a laugh with that line?"

"Of course.

He started the line. Just before the punch line, he took a long drag on his cigar. Then, through the smoke, he delivered the "punch" in typical Burnsian fashion. It was a good laugh, but I said I couldn't do it.

"Why?" he demanded indignantly.

"I don't smoke."

George stared at me balefully for a minute, then smiled. "Aww . . . go talk to your horse."

The first show was previewed before a full studio audience with George doing the warm-up. The audience's enthusiastic reaction to him was recorded, and that became our natural laugh track.

The show premiered on January 7, 1961. The reviews and reception were even better than we expected.

No matter how many shows you do, you never forget that first one. I remember watching the opening show with Larry Keating at the home of that great veteran actor William Conrad, better known in later days as the heavyweight protagonist in the popular series "Jake and the Fatman."

Bill's own television series was going off the air, and ours was just beginning. As he watched the debut of "Mister Ed," he turned to Larry and me and said, "Well, it looks as if you fellows will be working together for a long, long time."

He was partly correct. The series did endure for a long time, but dear Larry was to leave us tragically halfway through our run.

As those early weeks rolled by, my admiration for our trainer Lester Hilton grew enormously. He worked quietly, quickly, and efficiently. A typical lonesome cowboy, he was a man of few words. He never used two words if one would do. And even that one he used sparingly.

After the fourth or fifth show, he began to confide in me more, and eventually we became close friends. He would let me in on the little tricks he used to get Ed to perform certain movements.

There were even times he called upon me to help him. While he was busy getting Ed to "talk," I was shown how to touch the horse surreptitiously in certain spots so that he would turn his head in the right directions.

Lester told me that one of the biggest challenges wasn't getting Ed to do things, but letting him know when *not* to do them. Ed was quick to learn to pick up the phone, open doors and drawers. But the real trick was to teach him to do these things only at a specific time.

When Lester discovered that I didn't know the first thing about riding a horse, he insisted I come out to his place for lessons. There

"Okay, you got me all
dressed up, but where's a
horse going to go
in a tuxedo?"

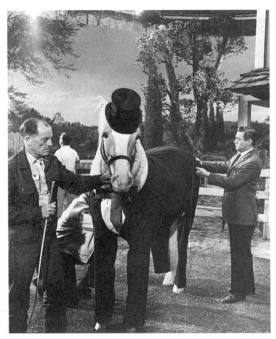

I learned to ride Ed. Like most horses, Ed was a bit lazy and reluctant to respond quickly to orders. He also sensed that in me he had a novice on his back. So while I was in the saddle, he was in the driver's seat.

To preserve Ed's mouth for his speaking chores, Lester didn't use a bit. Instead, he instructed me to use a hackamore, a rope rein which goes around the horse's muzzle. Finally I stopped using even that. I found that Ed—once he got used to my voice—responded more quickly if I just said "Stop," "Go," "Turn." After all, he was an actor.

This feeling of Ed as a fellow actor rather than a horse was becoming very strong in my thoughts.

On the show following the pilot, which is usually the first show of the series, I learned what it is like to work like a horse. Ed learned to work like a star. All eyes were on him. His every whim and wish were given conscientious consideration.

I realized that my performance in every take must be the best I could give, because if the horse performed properly, that was a "print." As a result, no matter how many times we had to repeat a scene, I must be at peak performance. This can be tiring.

We generally shot the scenes featuring just Ed and me on the first day of a week's shooting. There were many long, exhausting days. As a result, when I got home at night, there was very little dinner, no talk, just time to read the scenes for the following day, then sleep.

Not that Ed wasn't good at his job. But on a new show there are so many probable and possible glitches when a crew is learning to work together that retakes are a part of the process. Thankfully, Ed almost always performed his actions perfectly on the first shot.

However, sometimes a light might flicker, the focus wasn't exact, or I might not hit my mark exactly right. In each case, it meant another take. After two or three repetitions, Ed seemed to think that he was at fault. He would become confused and attempt to change his action. Then we were all in trouble.

One of those changes left a lasting impression on me. The scene opened with me working at my desk when the phone rang. Ed came over to me, nudged my arm, then picked up the phone in his teeth.

He did it perfectly on the first shot. However, the camera operator wasn't satisfied with his angle, so we started take two. Again Ed performed perfectly, nudging my arm and picking up the phone. But again there was a technical problem.

Now Ed was becoming confused. Arthur called out, "We'll get it this time. Action!"

I was the one who got it! Ed walked in, nudged the phone, and picked up my *arm* in his teeth. I let out a yelp that stopped the shooting on the next stage. Poor Ed was so upset that he couldn't work for the rest of the day, which was okay, because neither could I.

Yes, working with Ed was a little difficult for me at times. An actor working with an animal has to be letter perfect with his lines and continually on top of his performance, because if the animal

"I know it embarrassed Wilbur, but horses just like to kiss."

gets it right first time, that's a print—even if the actor is not completely satisfied.

One day I was a little tired and felt that I could have done a bit better in a particular shot. "Arthur," I said to the director. "I'd like to take that again. I think I could do it much better."

Arthur answered, "Sorry, Alan, I wasn't looking at you. The horse was perfect."

On this same show, a custom was established which exemplified the love and respect the cast and crew had for our star.

In one uninterrupted take, Ed had to cross from his stall to my letter file, open the drawer, remove a bunch of carrots, walk over and drop them on my desk, return to his stall, and shut the door.

We all realized that getting a horse to perform this sequence and also let go of a bunch of carrots, which he adored, was an almost-impossible challenge. Yet Ed did it, and in one take! Everyone watching burst into spontaneous applause.

Ed took the accolade with his usual composure. Glancing off-stage, I noticed trainer Lester was panting and sweating as if he had just run a three-minute mile.

Lester deserved a share of that enthusiastic applause which, from that day on, echoed through the sound stage every time Ed turned in a picture-perfect performance.

I learned something else from that first show. If the horse showed the least suggestion of fatigue, it was a wrap. No more shooting. Go home.

The human members of the cast could have dehydration, nervous prostration, or broken limbs—but we were asked to give it one more try. Not so our star. One yawn, and it was home and mother. We all agreed with that rule. After all, Ed was our bread and butter, and we loved him.

There were certain rules to be followed when Ed held center stage. Any activity around him had to be kept to a minimum because either his head or eyes would follow the slightest movement or distraction.

When he and I worked in a two-shot, I could never make any

"This was our very first publicity picture. Notice Wilbur couldn't even afford a tie. Notice I couldn't afford anything!"

hand or body gestures. I had to stand perfectly motionless and simply use facial expressions to emphasize or compliment the script.

At first I felt restrained and awkward, but soon discovered that the lift of an eyebrow or the twitch of the mouth can express much more than shoulder shrugging or arm waving. After all, there are more muscles in the face than in the rest of the body combined, and we don't use them nearly enough. Especially for smiling.

When we were shooting on the sound stage, Rocky Lane stood at the edge of the set with a microphone and script in front of him.

As soon as he started to read Ed's lines, Lester would activate Ed's mouth and I, of course, responded solely to Ed. This became such a natural activity that, after a while, I really felt that Ed and I were carrying on conversations.

This seems like the proper place for a few words about Ed's

speaking ability and how he did it. I have heard and read so many theories: they use electricity; his lips are wired; it's animation.

All wrong. I won't divulge every detail about the actual method because it was Lester's invention, but I must say that it involved nothing painful or irritating.

It was a little like having peanut butter stuck under your top lip and then trying to get rid of it. But the amazing thing with this trick was how Lester uncannily got Ed to do it on cue and stop at the right time.

By our second season, Ed was so adept at his lip movements that as soon as he heard me stop talking, he would start jawing. One day, while Lester and I were riding and talking together, Lester suddenly broke out laughing.

"Look at Ed," he pointed. "His lips are moving." Evidently Ed was so used to responding to my voice that he was joining in our conversation!

Lester pointed out that our threesome was very important. "You see, I'm the father image. I have to scold him and sometimes even punish him. Your job is to have motherly appeal."

This was proved true many times. Though Ed was docile and obedient, occasionally he could turn downright lazy. Then Lester would have to crack the whip.

This would shock Ed so much that he would sidle over to me and put his huge quivering chin on my shoulder so I could comfort and reassure him. But that's all it was—a crack of the whip. Just a sound. Never, never, never was Ed struck, or otherwise mistreated.

Lester brought Ed to the studio in a white horse trailer. Painted on both sides was the greeting: "Hello, I'm Mister Ed!"

I would often drive behind them along the Hollywood Freeway en route to the studio. It was great to see the faces of the usually sullen early-morning workers suddenly light up with joy. They would honk and wave and sometimes join the procession.

A few years before he passed away, I met the extremely funny Ted Knight, who created the brilliant character Ted Baxter on the

"Home after a hard day and Les Hilton is asleep in the trailer. You can't see, but I'm driving."

"Mary Tyler Moore Show." He told me that when he and his family first arrived in Hollywood they were a little in awe of the glamour and gilt, especially since he was a lowly character actor at the time.

One day Ted was driving with his family on the Hollywood Freeway when one of his children yelled, "Look, Dad, it's Mister Ed!"

There was the trailer with Ed's tail flowing majestically in the breeze. I was driving close behind. Ted said that they all waved, and I smiled and waved back.

Ted said he felt that the reassuring sight of their TV friends, Wilbur and Ed, driving merrily along made them feel at home and welcome in their new surroundings.

The top part of the trailer was open at the back. From my rear vantage point, I could always tell whether or not Ed was ready for work. If his tail was tucked down behind the tailgate, it meant he wasn't quite awake yet. But if it was outside the gate, flowing in the breeze, he was ready and eager. On those days, when we pulled

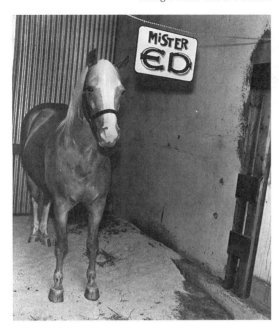

"This is my dressing room right next to Wilbur's. It'll look better once I get the drapes up."

onto the lot, he would begin stamping on the trailer floor, impatient to start acting.

Once out of his trailer, Lester took Ed behind the sound stage, where the actors' dressing rooms were located. At the end of the passageway was Ed's dressing room, a straw-filled paddock with his name painted next to a huge star.

When he wasn't working, Ed would stand in his stall, dozing quietly. But when he heard footsteps coming down the passage toward him, he would slowly turn his head to greet the visitor and gaze at him or her with his huge brown eyes.

With this famous star staring curiously and expectantly, the visitor usually felt obligated to make some response. Some of their responses were quite funny.

Ed's stall was right outside my dressing room, so I could hear the whole episode unfold. First the footsteps. Then they would slow up as they saw Ed staring at them. Then they would stop.

"Gee, you're Mister Ed. How are you?" a voice would say.

There was a pause, and I knew Ed was turning away from them and going back to his chewing or dozing. Then there would be a sound of footsteps hurrying along.

I met people later who confided sheepishly that they just didn't know how to handle meeting a star for the first time. "I didn't know what to say," most confessed.

People watching was part of Ed's naturally inquisitive nature. Every animal trainer I have spoken to has told me that the two qualities necessary in a theatrical animal are docility and inquisitiveness.

Ed had another quality that was a blessing to work with. He had an aura of total calm and serenity. Not always, of course, but most of the time, and especially when it really counted.

This inborn tranquillity was demonstrated perfectly on our first show. I was sitting in my chair off camera, desperately learning my lines. After all, it was the opening show, I didn't know the director too well, the crew was new and, for that particular job, I was still an unknown quantity. For an actor this is enough for the glands to start manufacturing flop sweat.

Lester was sitting next to me holding the rope attached to Ed's harness. Suddenly a huge light bulb the size of a volleyball fell from one of the lamps above us.

It hit the deck not six feet from us with the sound of a howitzer. I dropped my script. My knee-jerk muscle reflex lifted me six inches off the chair. Lester's dangling cigarette fell from his mouth.

We all turned toward our precious Ed—some to grab him, some to get out of his way in the expected panic-stricken stampede.

Incredibly, Ed's reaction was a slow Greta Garbo head-turn toward the offending noise. He assessed the situation, didn't understand it, then turned back to his dozing. Anything beyond his comprehension was outside his interest.

The only time I saw Ed stiffen with emotion was when a crowd of children came on the set, saw Ed, and surrounded him. They were oohing, aahing, touching, loving him.

Their sounds confused him, but he recognized their love for him.

"No matter how I disguised myself, somehow Wilbur always recognized me."

He was frozen in place, but not from fright. It was obvious that he didn't want to move and possibly step on one of these little feet. He remained motionless until the children were led away. Then he relaxed and began to stamp around.

One day a group of children surrounded me as I signed autographs for them, ignoring Ed for a few moments. Rocky Lane (Ed's voice) walked over quietly and stood behind the horse's head.

"Hey, Wilbur," he yelled. "Why don't the kids want my autograph?"

Immediately the children turned from me and rushed to Ed, holding out photographs and autograph books for him to sign.

A quick-thinking property man found some carbon paper, and we had Ed stamp out some "hoof-o-graphs." I hope some of those children kept their souvenirs because they must be worth something today.

Here I must add that, although I'm not particularly farsighted when it comes to investments, I did see the value of Mister Ed

"I told Wilbur: 'I don't go in a boat without my life-jacket and Dramamine.' "

memorabilia. So every time Ed had his shoes replaced—about every six weeks—I grabbed up the old ones and saved them.

I wasn't profitmongering. Whenever some responsible charity asked me for souvenirs or auction items, I would remove the nails, sand the horseshoes smooth, apply gilt, and was able to donate beautiful golden horseshoes. I guess Ed's feet are trotting through many a den throughout America. I trust the owners keep toasting him.

Ed's personal habits on the stage were also exemplary. I once visited the set of a TV western, and the sound stage looked and smelled like a camel's outhouse. Ed would never dream of defiling the set. He had too much respect for his fellow actors.

We always knew when nature was beckoning urgently. Ed's eyes would open wildly. His pupils seemed to dilate. Most times his heavy-duty functions were attended to right onstage, with the help of a wrangler who would simply lift up his tail and hold out a bucket. Our stage six was always accident-free.

Urination was another matter. Ed just couldn't bring himself to pee on the stage or in public. He would control himself until his eyes widened and started rolling.

Lester would lead him quickly offstage to his stall where, in privacy, the function would be performed in private, far from prying eyes.

Lester had many practical theories as to why Ed had such fastidious bathroom habits, but I prefer to think it was simply because Ed was a gentleman.

This was clearly demonstrated one day when we were shooting on the beach at Malibu. Ed's eyes were widening considerably and Lester informed our director of the impending mini-crisis.

"Can you hold it till we finish this one short shot?" Arthur asked Lester.

"I can, but I don't know about Ed," Lester replied.

"Let's try. We don't want to lose the sun."

Lester came to me. "Keep a good hold on him, Alan," he cautioned. "If he gets loose, there's nothing to stop him between here and the Pacific Coast Highway. That could be dangerous."

We began the scene, but my grip on his halter slackened for a split second. That's all it took. Ed pulled away and took off, disappearing through a clump of bushes. Lester raced toward the highway to head him off. The rest of us bolted into the bushes in pursuit of our star.

As we searched desperately for him, I heard loud guffaws coming from behind one of our portable dressing rooms. I hurried over and saw the reason for the laughter. Ed was standing behind the portable lavatories, gratefully relieving himself in the tall grass. Once relieved, he ambled back to the set, and we continued with the scene.

There's one last incident, and only real "accident" on this somewhat-indelicate subject which I recall—not to titillate, but simply to illustrate the truth of the theatrical adage, "The show must go on."

We were shooting a scene in which Ed was standing in a huge

"The famous bathtub scene. I was embarrassed."

vat filled with soapy water. I was on a ladder next to him, scrubbing his back. At a certain juncture Ed was to hop out of the tub. Then I would lose my balance and fall into the water. Messy shots like this are always filmed at the end of the day.

The tub was filled, Ed got in, I climbed the ladder, the camera began rolling, and the scene began. I had hardly started scrubbing when I noticed Ed's eyes widen and roll just a little. He had to go.

Before the wrangler could reach him with the bucket for his heavy-duty business, Ed lifted his tail and filled the tub with little floating globes. It was not picked up by the camera, but everyone on the set saw it. Now they were waiting to see what I would do.

At times like this, an actor's mind covers all the angles. It's not that he's particularly clever, it's a natural theatrical reaction.

I realized that the camera had not caught any of that extraneous, unexpected activity. I also realized that if I didn't go ahead with the scene, it would mean emptying, cleaning, and refilling the tub, easily an hour's work.

It was now five-thirty. The crew had had a long day and wanted to go home. I was tired. Worst of all, Ed was tired. Today was Friday, so we would have to postpone the scene until next week.

To hell with it.

I gave Ed his cue. He leaped out of the water. I held my breath, pursed my lips tightly, and fell into the tub.

The scene was completed. The day was saved. The crew was grateful, but wouldn't come near me. Somebody turned my shower on, and I rushed in, clothes and all. After scrubbing myself for what seemed to be an hour, I emerged clean.

Driving home behind Ed's trailer that night, I couldn't help asking myself, "Is this what happens when your costar is a horse?"

I answered my own question: "I've taken a lot more crap than this from some actors. Besides, Ed is my buddy."

3

A Winner All the Way!

January 1961: "Mister Ed" goes on the air and is hailed as an instant hit!

Everyone involved in the creation of the show was riding the crest of the wave, looking forward to a long, successful run. Me too—it's a great feeling to be part of a winning team.

Toward the end of the season we were even more ecstatic as our ratings kept building at a tremendous pace.

That is why we were all dumbstruck when the hammer fell at the end of our first year.

"'Mister Ed' is being taken off the air!" we were told. Unbelievable! Here we all were—part of a hit show that hadn't made it.

—The Avanti hadn't made it.

—The Studebaker Company couldn't afford the show.

—Steve Mudge's creative promotion, which had been hyped as the "sales coup of the year," had failed.

A few weeks after that bombshell dropped, our production big-gies, Al Simon and Marty Ransohoff, then president of Filmways, were having lunch at the Bel-Air Hotel in Westwood, trying des-perately to figure out what one does with a hit show when there is no place for it.

Sitting at an adjoining table were a group of CBS executives, engrossed in their own problems—namely, their program schedule for the next year.

Suddenly in walked James Aubrey, the CBS network program director. He greeted Al and Marty, then sat with them at their table.

"What's happening?" Aubrey asked them.

Al filled him in. "We have a hit show called "Mister Ed," but we have no place to put it." You must remember that "Mister Ed" was a syndicated show with no single network affiliation.

Aubrey was no slouch. He had a Sunday evening which was in trouble. The ratings for "Lassie" had been dropping off, which resulted in Ed Sullivan's ratings suffering. And Sunday night was CBS's greatest hope.

Aubrey reached in his pocket and took out a program schedule, studied it for a moment and asked, "How would you like Sunday night at seven o'clock?"

Al's and Marty's jaws dropped in unison. They nodded their ap-proval silently.

Aubrey gestured across to his frazzled executives at the next ta-ble: "Put "Mister Ed" in Sunday at seven."

And that was that.

It probably wasn't as happenstance as it sounds. A shrewd pro-grammer, Jim Aubrey knew full well that "Mister Ed" was pulling in the audiences.

So it wasn't just an impulsive gamble he was taking. He also figured that "Mister Ed" could be a shot in the arm for CBS Sun-day nights, lifting the network out of the Sunday doldrums.

And he was right. Sunday night became CBS's big evening again. "Mister Ed's" strong shoulders pulled their fat out of the fire.

"Mister Ed" cast members traveled to New York to take part in CBS's annual announcement of its fall 1963 lineup. We met with other cast members at the elevator before heading down to the grand ballroom. We were all in great spirits, but I'll never forget what happened next.

While waiting, Larry Keating took me aside and said, "I haven't told anyone else, Alan, but I just found out I have a few months to live. I think you should know so that when we work together in the fall you can be ready."

That September we shot our memorable episode in which Mister Ed teaches the L.A. Dodgers how to play baseball. It was probably our funniest and most spectacular show of the season. All the great Dodgers were part of it: manager Leo Durocher, catcher Johnny Roseboro, Sandy Koufax, with the rest of the team enjoying Ed's coaching.

Ed's first time at bat, he hit a homer and started to run the bases. Being a horse, he ignored the dirt track and headed for the soft grass. The stadium was quite new at the time and, as he ran, his hooves tore up clods of freshly planted sod, which flew through the air in his wake like green spray.

By the time he slid home—which was a sight in itself—Buddy Bavazzi, the general manager of the Dodgers, ran out on the field in a lather. Their opening game was a week away, and here was the infield grass looking like an exploded mine field.

It's times like this you're glad you're not a producer, but simply an actor or a horse. So Ed and I took off quietly, leaving Arthur and Al Simon to do the placating and replanting.

The joy of this good show was quickly replaced when, in the next scene, I had to help Larry Keating up off the ground. As I lifted him, he gripped my hands hard. I stared into his eyes. They were usually twinkling and mischievous, but now they looked empty.

"I'm glad this is my last shot, Alan, because I think it's the last we'll do together," he said.

We took the next week off while Larry rested. My family spent the weekend relaxing at the Newport Inn. Coming down for break-

Above left: "Wilbur tried to umpire, Leo Durocher threw *him* out!"

Above right: "Johnny Roseboro wants me to take the bat, but I have a better system for base running. "

" I enjoyed playing against the Dodgers. Especially Sandy Koufax."

"First you kiss the catcher,"

"Then you *run*!"

"Headin' home!"

"He missed the tag!"

"Weeee!"

"Safe by a nose."

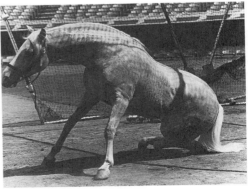

"The toughest part is getting up!"

"No one could say that Wilbur didn't rule the roost."

fast, I went to the newsstand for a paper. On the front page was a picture of Larry. I just couldn't buy it. I knew.

Larry couldn't be replaced, so his wife, played by Edna Skinner, was forced to leave the show because another husband for her would just be emotionally unacceptable to the audience.

Until this happened, we introduced the character of her brother, a songwriter, played by the late great Jack Albertson. But Jack, who later went on to greater stardom in the sitcom "Chico and the Man," had already committed himself to another comedy series and left us only after a few weeks.

New neighbors had to be found. A natural candidate was Wilbur's former army colonel and his wife, played by crusty character actor Leon Ames and the delightful Florence MacMichael.

Looking back at the actors who made guest appearances or supported us in the series is a delightful recollection. We were blessed with our guests.

George Burns, of course, was one of our first guests. What can you say about George without sounding like an echo? He was delightful, funny, and so easy to work with.

Sadly, on the same show, making her first TV appearance and perhaps her first theatrical appearance was the beautiful young actress Sharon Tate, one of the tragic victims of the infamous Charles Manson.

Zsa Zsa Gabor appeared on one of our early shows. Appropriately, she played the part of Zsa Zsa, which is all you can ask for and is all you need. She sure lived up to the public image she has created for herself.

As Zsa Zsa was playing an opulent movie star in this particular show, it was necessary to have her dressed for the role. For the most part, she wore her own gorgeous gowns—but then she got to thinking that the "Mister Ed" producers could afford to rent a full-length mink coat for her to toss over her shoulders.

At the end of the final day of shooting her scenes, Al Simon suddenly had an alarming premonition. When he heard that Zsa Zsa was leaving the lot, he alerted the front gate.

Sure enough, she was driving off with the mink which, in those days, was worth around $10,000, probably much, much more today.

"I'm sorry, dahling," she explained, totally unfazed at being stopped. "But most of the studios give me coats like this as gifts!"

Clint Eastwood was already a star in the successful "Rawhide" series but he owed Arthur Lubin a favor. So he kindly agreed to be one of our guests. He did a very funny part. He played himself, as one of our neighbors who agreed to help out as the director of my wife Carol's benefit show, a western spoof. Clint was a good sport and proved that the bigger they are, the nicer they are.

One of our most popular guests hadn't made any appearances for years until she visited Mister Ed. She was none other than Mae West, who told me that once she made up her mind to make a television appearance, she wanted to work only with the handsomest, biggest and strongest male in the medium. Who else but Mister Ed?

It's truly amazing how many popular personalities and stars com-

" Zsa Zsa is a guest and has on a ten-thousand-dollar mink coat. I'm the star, and I'm wearing the same old hair."

" From left: Carol (Connie Hines), Colonel (Leon Ames), Winnie (Florence MacMichael), Wilbur (Alan Young)."

Leon Ames

"Wilbur and I had matching hairstyles."

"The gang's all here! Wait, where am I?"

"Mae West was a guest on our show. For some silly reason I'm turning toward Wilbur. Go figure a horse."

"Wilbur showed Clint Eastwood how to do westerns. He sure caught on, didn't he?"

municated through their agents or friends that they would love to be guests on "Mister Ed." But our producers were very selective when it came to guest appearances. Though appreciating their interest and sincerity, Al Simon wanted to protect this novel show from exploitation.

The show's selective policy regarding guest appearances got screwed up just once as far as I can remember. Our otherwise-very-competent producer-director Arthur Lubin was responsible, much to Al Simon's chagrin.

Arthur knew little or nothing about sports and couldn't care less who was who in the arena of athletics. So I was surprised to get a phone call from him one day: "Alan, you know about sports. Guess who I have booked as a guest star!"

Since Arthur had been responsible for two of our most famous guests, Clint Eastwood and Mae West, I knew he must have a biggie.

"I have booked the boxing champion of the world," he said triumphantly.

"You got Jersey Joe Walcott?" I gasped.

"Who?"

"Jersey Joe Walcott."

"Now why would I want him, whoever he is?" Arthur was getting irritated. He didn't like people confusing him.

"Arthur, Walcott is the boxing champion of the world."

"Of course he isn't. It's Ricky Starr."

"Who?"

"Ricky Starr, the world champion. And he's going to be on the show. I just talked to Lou, and he's writing the script.

After Arthur hung up, I called Al Simon and discovered that Arthur's discovery was, in fact, the world wrestling champion—at least, the world as far west as Omaha. We had to move fast—he would hold the title only until the end of the month.

Al had some footage of Ricky Starr's wrestling "act," which he screened proudly for us. We all had to admit it was extremely funny. The young man had been a college champion and also had studied ballet. He had merged his two talents into a hilarious performance.

He would enter the ring, do some barre exercises and then perform a few entrechats, then prance around the ring throwing tiny ballet slippers to the audience. His antics went unnoticed by his huge, villainous opponent who studiously kept his back to the center of the ring.

Ricky would suddenly set his sights at his opponent, perform a series of spins as he approached him gracefully, then pat him gently on the shoulder. When the gorilla turned to face him, Ricky threw him a kiss and spun gracefully back to his own corner.

The villain was furious and the match began. He tried to kill Ricky, who performed graceful ballet escapes and then kicked the hell out of the brute, but always *en pointe.*

To tremendous applause, Ricky performed his routine on our show. Even when it was all over, dear well-meaning Arthur never admitted that we had not played host to the boxing champion of the world. But we had to admit that, accidentally or not, he had booked a funny guest.

It was the simple relationship between Wilbur and Mister Ed that was the backbone of the series. This buddy-type of friendship is clearly delineated in the following scenes:

INTERIOR BARN—DAY

Wilbur is working at his desk. Ed has a newspaper in front of him and a pencil in his mouth, as he is doing the crossword puzzle.

> ED: Hmmm. Three-letter word meaning "rodent."
> ED: Addison?
> WILBUR: (taking the pen out of Ed's mouth)
> Don't be so funny. The word is r-a-t.
> ED: Okay, don't spell it. I may be dumb, but I'm not stupid.

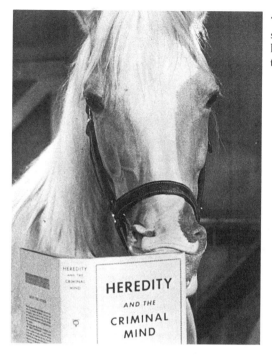

"I try to keep up to date on stuff. You never know how long this acting gig is going to last."

WILBUR (sighs): Just what have you got against Mr. Addison, Ed?

ED: Mom taught us kids never to trust a man with a mustache.

WILBUR: Oh, that's ridiculous. That's like my not trusting a horse because he has a tail.

ED: Please—let's not split hairs.

WILBUR: Ed, you should try to love your neighbor. This would be a better world to live in if people learned to love each other. Now—

ED (wearily): Okay, finish the sermon and pass the plate.

WILBUR (annoyed): Don't you get fresh with me. When I talk to you I expect you to listen. Is that clear?

ED (scared): Holler, but don't hit!

FADE OUT

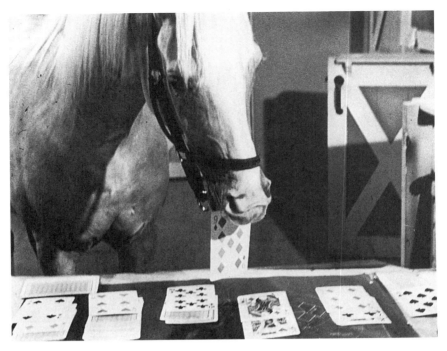

"Let's see . . . the red nine goes on the . . . don't tell me."

In another show, Ed had talked Wilbur into taking him to Mexico with Carol. However, Carol said she would not spend her vacation with a horse. Wilbur now has to break the news to Ed. As he enters the stall, Ed is eating.

> WILBUR: Hi, Ed.
>
> ED (gaily): A buenos dias to you amigo.
>
> WILBUR (conning): Ed, I've been thinking about Mexico. You know, with the change of climate, you're going to feel real logy. Besides, the food is different, the water, the altitude. Maybe you should reconsider.
>
> ED: First time I ever heard a man tout a horse.
>
> WILBUR: Ed, believe me, I tried, but Carol just doesn't want you along.

"After a good night's rest, I eat breakfast . . . the mattress."

ED (putting it on): Okay, leave me alone on my birthday.

Wilbur is touched by the tone of Ed's voice.

WILBUR: Now Ed, pull yourself together. It's only for three days. Besides, Carol started to cry and when I see someone cry, I just can't say "no."

Tears are streaming down Ed's face. He sniffs pathetically.

WILBUR: Okay, okay—don't cry, Ed. I'll tell Carol you're going with us.

He rushes out.

ED: Anything she can do I can do better!

FADE OUT

In this show, Ed has convinced Wilbur that he is suffering terribly because he has to sleep standing up. Finally he wheedles Wilbur into buying him a real "people" bed. The next morning, Wilbur enters the barn.

> WILBUR: Hi, Ed. Feel better today?
> ED (very chipper): In the pink, Wilbur. It's good to be on my feet again.
> WILBUR: How'd you like the bed?
> ED: What a night. When I was covered, my tail wasn't—and when my tail was covered, I wasn't.
> WILBUR: So you didn't like the bed, huh?
> ED: No, but the mattress was delicious!

FADE OUT

It was nearing the end of our fifth season and contract-renewal time. I had signed the original contract for very little money, certainly by today's standards. At the time, I was grateful for the steady work, but now I saw an opportunity for improvement.

Filmways Company generously agreed to my new contract. And thanks to an alert lawyer who negotiated my contract, I received a piece of the action. Not a percentage of the show which, through "creative bookkeeping," can result in a piece of nothing, but a percentage of the producer's profits. I think this loophole was closed shortly afterward, so perhaps I just squeezed through.

They also agreed to have me direct a certain number of the shows each season. I think most actors want to try their hand at directing, if only to prove to themselves that they can (or cannot) do it.

My directorial opportunity came very swiftly. Arthur Lubin was vacationing, and his substitute director was called away in the

"Wilbur can't even ride a camera. He's missed the seat completely!"

"This was Wilbur's first day as a director, and Connie brought him a cup of tea. For that she got six close-ups."

middle of our show. I was handed the reins, so to speak.

It could have been a traumatic experience had it not been for our ace cameraman and a meticulous, efficient script supervisor. If those two people are good, the director's job is a cinch. If not, the director has an industrial-sized headache.

The cameraman, Archie Dalzalle, was a jolly, speedy artist who loved his work and his fellow workers. Maggie Lawrence, our script supervisor, had an eagle eye for detail as well as a keen sense of the artistic.

In all, I directed half a dozen shows, and the crew made my job a joy. At the end of the season, I discovered two things: one— directing is easy, and two—I didn't like it.

I'm sure the impudent statement "directing is easy" needs some explanation. Directing an epic or mystery demands prodigious directorial and editing skills. Directing a comedy is easy.

Performing true comedy is the hardest area of our business, as most actors will admit. There's the oft-told story that when the great actor Edmund Gwenn was on his deathbed, he was visited by a friend, who sat silently beside him. Finally, noticing his arduous breathing, he asked. "Edmund, is it so hard?"

"No," Edmund said quietly. "Dying is easy. Comedy is hard."

Directing comedy is—or should be—much easier. Keep it simple and don't let complicated camera directions get in your way. What you see through the lens should be photographed without arty frills. Just capture the simplest details.

Charlie Chaplin's "bun dance" in his movie *The Gold Rush* is a perfect example of this delightful simplicity. This touching, brilliant piece of pantomime was shot straight on. No arty angles, no fancy lighting, no aesthetic cuts or editing.

Who would use opera glasses at a ballet to get a close-up of the feet, or mouth, or hands? The entire body is giving the message, so keep it all in view.

In comedy, as in most types of communication, the key word is "simplicity." The fewest words should be used in a gag line, the fewest movements in a physical portrayal.

As Charlie Chaplin said, "If you're doing something funny, don't be funny doing it."

That's one of the secrets behind the success of "Mister Ed." The show never pretended to be something it wasn't. It was the very essence of simplicity. And it worked!

PART 2

"Lips Don't Sweat"

4

In the Beginning

The wildest, most heathenish bands of ravagers in existence swept into my hometown. It was around 800 A.D., so I wasn't too concerned.

But there they were. Those Norse and Danish invaders, or Vikings (sons of the fjords), swarmed across the North Sea, in ships with graceful hulls and high-necked bows, which eventually resulted in the sea-lane being called "The Path of the Swans."

How coincidental that they should land at Newcastle-on-Tyne, often referred to as being "strictly for the birds."

It was here that the Vikings chose to begin their systematic ritual of arson and pillage. And here my ancestors were spared, as they had nothing to burn, and little worth stealing.

Two years after this invasion, the Vikings were being assimilated into the community when, suddenly, from the north, beyond Hadrian's Wall, swarmed the Picts.

These kilted savages who painted their bodies blue and puffed wailing battle-songs from bagpipes made from sheep bladders came burning and pillaging. Their hopes and bags deflated when they saw that my ancestors didn't have a pot to pillage, it's said that they took up a collection, but this could be apocryphal. In any case many of the Picts actually liked Tyneside, and stayed. They, too, were soon assimilated into the community. The land around the banks of the River Tyne had been potently and continually impregnated with a strong Pict and Viking influence—a world of difference to the Englishmen of Saxon and Norman descent who preferred to reside farther south.

This influence can be discerned today in the language of the Tynesider from Jarrow to Whitley Bay to Newcastle. Listen to the talk in the High Street.

"Haddaway hinnie, wor yi gannin'?"

"Aam gannin' hyem."

"Wor yi bin?"

"Schyull."

In English, the aforementioned dialogue would read:

"Hi love, where are you going?"

"I'm going home."

"Where have you been?"

"School."

A visitor from no more than fifty miles away finds it nigh impossible to understand the conversation of "Geordie," a nickname given them by the fiercely independent Scots from the north who saw the Tynesiders as allies of England's hated King George I.

The Geordie is insular or friendly, gentle or wild, depending on the whim of the wind or the cut of the jib. His bloodline is seasoned with a variety of unpredictable emotional responses that would have Dear Abby calling her sister for advice.

British breweries vary the strength of their beverages to suit the demands of the workingman in various areas of the country. The strongest by far is supplied to the Tynesider. This is not a matter for pride nor shame, simply an indication of taste.

Lest the impression be left that the strength of the hop is the height of Tynesiders' intellect, it must also be noted that Tyneside

Dad and I in an early press photo.

was the birthplace of St. Bede the Venerable, a keen intellectual known as the "Father of English History."

As Samson's riddle states: "Out of the strong proceed the sweet."

So, out of the burning, pillage, and rape which clouds my ancestry comes a polyglot people: singed, poor, but smilingly serene.

In the late 1800s the Cathcart clan emerged from the quiet, scholarly dignity of Edinburgh, Scotland. They settled in Tynemouth where later, John Cathcart Young, the youngest son, met Florence Pinckney, as direct a descendant of Geordies as eight rapacious invasions would allow. Florence was my mother.

Mother was orphaned at sixteen. This left her with a choice of becoming a barmaid in her brother's pub—or marriage. Since working as a barmaid in a dockside tavern is like being a bowl of guacamole dip at a Cinco de Mayo party, Mother opted for whatever John Young had to offer.

As early as 1912, John had been planning a trip to the New World to seek his fortune. But along came Mother—and she corraled him before he could embark.

In no time at all, they established their own connubial new world. And my big sister Hattie and World War I exploded into existence simultaneously.

Archduke Ferdinand and the assassin's gun were cooling off to-

"'Gentlemen marry brunettes."

gether when Dad packed his bag, kissed his little family farewell, and took off for the recruiting station like a goosed gazelle. Having ridden on the North Shields ferry any number of times it was only natural that Dad should enlist in His Majesty's Navy. It was even more natural that he should volunteer for submarine duty for, as he put it to the recruiting officer, "This way I can strike at the heart of those damn Belgians!"

At first the officer was puzzled, but then kindly pointed out that the Belgians were on our side. It was the Germans who were our enemies. This was acceptable to Dad, who confessed that he had enlisted so fast that he hadn't been quite sure of the ground rules.

"But if that's who the king is after, I'm with him!" he declared. Then, picking up his papers and throwing the officer a smart, incorrect salute, he marched off proudly.

Reaching the door, he paused and turned back to the officer. "I'd still keep my eye on those Belgians," Dad warned.

Dad's attempt to strike at the enemies' heart took a detour past the liver. He was shipped to a naval observation post in northern Scotland. It consisted of a two-room hut clinging bravely to a rocky cliff, exposed on all sides to paralyzing gale-force winds. It's doubtful that the German High Command even knew that spot existed.

But never was water stared at more intently. The slightest change in atmosphere or a strange bird flying overhead brought the admiralty an immediate red phone call from Dad.

For four years, Dad kept this lonely, faithful vigil with never a word of complaint, until finally honorably discharged. With a family to think about, Dad turned his thoughts and abilities toward the world of commerce. With his usual keen business sense, Dad decided to open a small defense plant, overlooking the fact that the war had ended two months before. In fact, he succeeded in losing his shirt at least nine years before the stock-market crash.

Pausing only to put the blame on the Belgians, Dad started in again, this time as an assistant bookkeeper for a shipyard in North Shields, Northumberland. It wasn't the type of work he had planned on, but after Mother whispered in his ear that the family was about to be increased, he decided that the equivalent of $12 a week was the better part of valor.

And I was born. There is nothing more to say about that. It would be marvelous to report that at the very instant a star flashed in the heavens, and an old gypsy woman shrieked the ominous prediction, "Watch for a tall palomino horse with a big mouth."

But no. I was just born. It was simply a relief to my mother. And, as far as I was concerned, the only alternative at the time.

"The *Cairnmona,* a 20,000-ton freighter, en route from Edinburgh, Scotland to Montreal, Canada, ran aground on Heath Point, Anticosti Island, early this morning. A dense fog hinders rescue operations."—News Item.

This report meant little to the Canadians reading it over their cheery breakfast tables. But, to the shivering Youngs, headed for a new life in the New World, huddled in blankets and crouched by the lifeboat, it was the most momentous event since Moses came downhill carrying the tablets.

The crash was a big one. I had just climbed back into the bunk to keep warm and was clutching a slice of bread, thick with

"I see a talking horse in your future."

strawberry jam, when the impact of the crash tossed me onto the cabin floor.

Mother hurried into the cabin. Her face was chalk white—an improvement. For the entire trip it had been a deep shade of green.

"The ship is sinking!" she screamed. As an impressionable five-year-old, I was more concerned with my squashed bread and jam. But throwing a blanket over our heads, Mother started dragging her endangered offspring topside.

On deck the atmosphere was tense. I have a vivid recollection of Dad, always ready to perform his duty, standing stiffly at attention by the rail holding a fire ax. What he intended doing with it was a mystery to everyone.

Dad dropped the ax and started strapping life preserves on everyone in sight. Somehow he put my legs through the shoulder straps. When he finished, I was wearing a cork diaper. Unless I could breathe through my feet, I was a goner.

"Now stay where you are until I come back!" Dad ordered, lashing us to the mast. "I've got to help the crew lower the boats. Sing hymns or something."

Until then, I had regarded the whole experience as a fascinating break in a rather monotonous sea voyage. But now, being tied to a mast in an upside-down life jacket was just too much to bear. We were enveloped in a thick, chilling fog which seeped through our nostrils and grabbed our throats. I began crying my eyes out.

After what seemed like eons, our ordeal was over. A high tide got us afloat again. And the good ship *Cairnmona*, somewhat the worse for wear, chugged up the St. Lawrence River to Quebec City, where we disembarked.

I was told later that the *Cairnmona* gave up the ghost and sank shortly after that. I really didn't care. At least she waited until we got off.

What a welcome to North America!

No people have fought more fiercely for—and sung more songs about—their country than the Scots. Yet it would seem they can't

In the military pipe band. When I played, the soldiers stood still but four bagpipes ran away.

wait to leave it. In fact, the farther they get from Scotland, the louder they sing about loving and missing it.

Nevertheless, no country has brought forth more explorers, colonizers, and immigrants per capita than Scotland. Travel to the Arctic tundra, and you'll come across Nanook MacDougal fishing through a hole in the ice. Take a stroll across Tierra del Fuego, and there you'll meet Sanchez MacKay.

The average Scot can't wait to leave his bonnie wee hoose strapped to a barren, windswept rock, and his neighbors, the MacLaughlins and the Munroes, and emigrate to Canada. There he searches out a barren, windswept rock, builds a wee abode, and waits hopefully for the MacLaughlins and the Munroes. My father was no different.

He dragged our family kicking and screaming as far west as the railway would go, to the Pacific Ocean in British Columbia. We settled in a wee hamlet called Caulfield, up the road from an equally wee town called Dunderave (all named after Scottish vil-

" 'They say you don't have to toss the caber far. Just lift it.' Easy for him to say."

lages, of course). And there were our neighbors, the MacDonalds and the Weirs. For Dad, it was a home away from home.

I listen to comedians talk about small towns: "My hometown was so small we had only one yellow page! The only excitement on a Saturday night was to go down to the Hertz office and watch them rent the car!"

A telephone? A car? A radio? Those are signs of a metropolis, baby! Ever trap a skunk in your bedroom? Or go looking for moose tracks? Ever climb up a 100-foot fir tree to see if you can spot another house somewhere?

This was my new world. And, as an impressionable wee schoolboy, I loved every minute of my neighborhood. Walking through woods without seeing another soul, fishing for trout in crystal streams, lying on a bed of moss six inches thick, staring up at a blue sky through the branches of a pine tree . . . it was all so wonderful back then. Deprived? Don't you believe it!

Our home was a one-room "summer cottage" nestled on the

hillside on the west shore of Burrard Inlet. Facing us, far below, was the Georgia Strait, leading out into the Pacific Ocean. Behind us, the majestic, mountainous Pacific Range. The feeling of being "at the back of beyond" was overwhelming. We felt truly we were at the top of the world.

Our cottage was originally built for wealthier visitors from nearby Vancouver to spend weekend vacations. But money for recreation was hard to come by after the 1929 depression, and the city visitors stopped coming.

Five dollars a month rented one of these little beauties—which seems like almost nothing, until you realize that you were getting almost nothing.

The cottage was actually four walls and a floor. No heat, light, or plumbing. A wood stove supplied the heat. Kerosene lamps gave us light, and a short walk into the woods provided our toilet necessities.

One of the high points in our life was the weekly ritual of the family bath. Water hauled from a stream was heated on top of the stove, using every container available. The children got first whack at it, when the water was piping hot, then Mother, then Father.

An area the size of a two-car garage didn't allow a family of four much privacy, so Dad scraped up some discarded lumber and attached a lean-to at the side of the house. Add one army cot and this became my bedroom.

In the summer I would slide the cot out and sleep under the sky. In summer it stayed light until almost eleven at night, and then began to brighten up about two in the morning.

So there was much to watch all night . . . and the lost sleep could always be gained by an afternoon stretch-out on my mossy hill.

Back in the old country, Mother had been the respected assistant to the local midwife. Since money was short, she decided to get back into the baby-delivering profession.

One of the first babies she delivered was the child of our local health inspector, Mr. Gracey, who, like most civil servants in those days, was underpaid and also short on cash. So Mother's fee was arranged on the barter system.

But, as Mr. Gracey didn't have anything worth bartering, he graciously appointed my father "Special Assistant to the Health Inspector (carcass cremator) Caulfield division."

This impressive job title demands explanation.

The Georgia Strait, which our cottage overlooked, was the place where the Pacific current from Japan and the Arctic current from Alaska converged. Because of this, it teemed with the most diversified ocean life imaginable. Octopus, shark, sea anemone, all kinds of marine life generally found in tropical waters thrived here, mingling with walrus, seals, and other creatures which reflected the Arctic environment.

Because of this zoological hodgepodge, dead whales, sharks, and sea lions washed up on our beaches from time to time, stinking up the place to high heaven.

It was the Special Assistant's duty to patrol the beaches and look for these unfortunate creatures, in father's case an all too brief two-mile stretch of shoreline. His job was to burn the remains. For each funeral pyre, he was to be paid five dollars.

Father wasn't optimistic about this career. Mr. Gracey had told him up front that a paltry one or two animals a month was par for that particular stretch of beach. But jobs were hard to come by, and this was the best section he could give Dad for the time being.

A whole week went by, and Dad had found and burned only one cadaver. He searched in vain for more, but the beaches were sweet-smelling.

But the following week, he couldn't believe his eyes. As far as he could see along his stretch of beach were dead carcasses: birds, beasts, fish. You name the critter, Dad's beach had 'em all!

Within an hour, ten wonderful fires were blazing along our shoreline. To the passing observer, it looked like a Normandy beachhead. To Dad, it spelled fifty dollars.

The following morning, more remains awaited Dad's disposal. And, for the rest of the week, at least two a day were to be found above the high-water mark. The job of Special Assistant (Carcass Division) was becoming a bonanza!

About the middle of the third week, a worried Mr. Gracey came to visit. "You've been quite busy, Mr. Young," he said. "How do you account for it?"

"Some underwater epidemic?" Dad volunteered.

"But it's strange that all the carcasses float onto *your* beach," Mr. Gracey pondered, scratching his head. "The other sections haven't had a carcass in a month."

On hearing this exchange, I sensed that Dad's lucrative employment was coming to an end. I knew—because I started it!

To help his job along, I had been going out with a buddy in a rowboat early every morning, scouting for carcasses.

We toured every island and inlet where we knew dead sea creatures washed ashore. Then we would tether them to a towline and ship them back to Dad's jurisdiction, dragging the bobbing corpses behind us surreptitiously like a string of putrescent pearls.

I knew Mr. Gracey was on to us—so Dad's gold rush had to end as fast as it began.

Ever philosophical, Father seemed glad the strange oceanic epidemic was over, and grateful that it had at least brought in enough money to see us through the winter. The money also encouraged Mother to move her family out of the woods and rent a home in the big city.

The big city was the municipality of West Vancouver, population: 3,000. Now it would be 3,004!

5

Bitten by the Bug

It was around the time of our move to the big city of West Vancouver that I became quite ill.

Two doctors agreed that the root problem was bronchial asthma, which from the age of ten to seventeen, kept me bedridden for at least four months a year.

My parents soon found that keeping a growing boy indoors was as futile as autographing a bowl of Jell-O.

On days when I could breathe fairly well, I would sneak out the window, change into my beloved soccer gear in the bushes, then rush off to Ambleside Park, our local soccer field, for a glorious two hours of playing my favorite game, usually in a pouring rain.

Breathless, soaking wet, but happy, I would sneak back home. No wonder I spent the next few nights fighting for breath. But it was worth it.

When Mother found out what I was up to, she insisted on taking me with her whenever she went on a job. When she had no midwife calls, Mother took jobs as a charwoman—a British euphemism for a cleaning lady.

Seeing my mother on her hands and knees scrubbing floors in the homes of some of my more affluent schoolmates left a searing impression on me. I suppose it was then I vowed that when I made money, she would never have to work or worry again.

My chronic illness turned out to be a blessing in disguise. Friends would bring me books, magazines, papers—anything with printing on it. I became an insatiable reader.

Perhaps due to my miserable condition, I leaned toward humor. Anything by Stephen Leacock or Robert Benchley was among my favorite reading. Then, when my eyes became too strained to read, I would lie back in bed and envision myself taking part in all the funny and exciting stories.

This daydreaming was my favorite childhood escape. I could build a castle in the air, fill the moat, and lift my drawbridge before Walter Mitty had dug his foundation.

My ability to make swift detours into the realms of unreality was a lifesaver for me at least two or three times a day. During my illness, I'd embark on mental adventures so engrossing that the physical pain and strain were forgotten for a while.

One of my adventures was to reenact a radio show of the night before. I played the lead, of course. Many times I was surprised to discover I could perform an entire sketch verbatim.

Jack Benny's show was my favorite, but Sunday was so filled with fabulous comedy and variety that it was a difficult choice.

Sunday brought Eddie Cantor, followed by Edgar Bergen, Charlie McCarthy and W. C. Fields, with Dorothy Lamour and Nelson Eddy as vocalists. Then Fanny Brice came on, followed by Jack Benny, then Fred Allen's full hour of brilliant character and comedy from New York.

Families sat together on Sunday from three in the afternoon until after dinner. They had more time together in one afternoon than today's families spend in a week.

Lying in bed listening to the various comedy shows, I began to

Candidly Hollywood

analyze the technique of gag writing. It is said, rightly or wrongly, that there are only seven or eight basic plots in fiction. The same rule of thumb applies to jokes. At first, the only talent of the gag writer is stealing. Then he learns to steal and adapt, known in the industry as "switching." He finally becomes so adept at this technique that he is eventually regarded as being original and innovative.

In no way is this meant to demean the art of comedy writing. To the contrary. If anyone thinks that writing humor or being a comedian is easy, just try it!

One of my first experiments with "switching" was with a line from Shakespeare, one of the greatest gag writers of all time, who described some boring event as being "As exciting as watching a thaw." I switched it to "As exciting as watching ice melt." This later became "As exciting as watching grass grow," or "Like watching paint dry."

Being a parlor comic is simple, but the distance between the party clown and the professional comedian is enormous.

Becoming a comedian is a constant, consuming obsession. It is a continual experiment. Write, rewrite, try, flop, retry, reflop, try, flop . . . succeed!

My first publicity shot in New York. I'm giving new meaning to the term Soda Jerk.

Another favorite learning ground for me was a daily radio show called "The British Empire Program," which featured top British recording stars. I would learn all the words and amuse family and friends, and anyone else who would listen, by imitating old-timers like Gracie Fields (before my voice broke), Harry Lauder, Bea Lillie, and Cecily Courtneidge. I loved their accents. In fact, I got so adept with accents that I could pinpoint what part of the British Isles someone came from after just a couple of words.

One day I was invited to give one of my parlor recitations at our local Caledonia Society, a Scottish organization. They gave me a choice of a fee or inviting my family for a free dinner of "mince and tatties" (ground beef and potatoes), a humble-but-favorite

Scots dish. I knew the fee would only be two or three dollars at most, so I invited my family to dine. I should have taken the cash.

This led to my first big-time appearance on a local radio show called "The Bathnight Revue," a two-hour Saturday-night potpourri of British entertainment aired from radio station CJOR in Vancouver.

Taking part were Scottish singers, English bar balladeers, and Welsh coloraturas. My contribution was Stanley Holloway's popular Lancashire monologue, "Albert and the Lion." The mixture of youth, a clever poem, and the fact that I followed a soprano who sang four flats no matter what the time or the weather resulted in my receiving terrific applause and a request for an encore.

"What's an encore?, I asked.

"They want you to perform again," the emcee said, smiling indulgently at the audience.

I didn't realize they wanted me to give them a different piece of material. "Albert and the Lion" was all I had ready, so I recited it all over again.

The audience evidently recognized a lost soul and laughed and applauded even more the second time. I was a hit and was booked as a regular performer on the show.

I was to discover that the years of studying comedy while bedridden were about to pay off. As a friend later said to me, "The testing times that happen aren't important of themselves. It's how we handle them when they happen. That's what's important!" Well, I had turned my trying, bedridden times into writing opportunities.

Once I wrote a ten-minute sketch and, when I was feeling all right, traveled to a Vancouver radio station to sell it. After sitting in a waiting room for an hour or so, the producer's secretary's sympathy overcame her, and she said, "Mr. Claringbull is too busy to see you. Just leave your script, and he'll be in touch." I left it and took off, grateful because she had accepted it, and also because I wasn't feeling very well.

That trip put me back in bed for a few days, but at the end of the week I listened to his program. They performed my sketch word for word, and I lay back in bed ecstatically. They had accepted my writing!

For several weeks I waited for a response from Mr. Claringbull. Maybe a thank-you note. Maybe even a payment. Nothing came. Thank God I had never learned the word "resentment." When you're at the bottom of the ladder, you learn to pick up your marbles and get back into the game.

Eight years later, I found out how retribution works. I was now in Toronto and had been writing and starring in my own show for a year when the telephone rang. "Hello, Alan, my name is Dick Claringbull. I'm producing a national variety radio show for the Canadian Red Cross, and we need someone to write it. There's no money involved, but could you donate a script?"

I wrote it. How could I refuse? The emcee for that show was a dear friend, Lorne Greene, one of Canada's greatest sons. After the show, a delighted Claringbull came up to me backstage at the McGill Street studio.

"Alan," he enthused, "how can I thank you?"

"You did—in Vancouver, six years ago. You used my first script. I was Angus Young then."

He remembered. His shoulders hunched and his stomach pulled in as if he had been belted. The message was clear to me: "Don't waste time trying to get even with people. Get ahead."

Becoming a professional entertainer was a great thrill for me. I remember those early days when I received my first pay for my first professional engagement in show business! I had been acting the clown for years, doing the silly things I loved to do—couldn't help doing. Now someone was paying me for it!

The fee for my four-minute monologue was three dollars. Dad put in a full day's tough manual labor at the shipyard for that kind of money. He stared unbelievingly at my envelope.

"Angus," he counseled. "You keep up with this talking business—because lips don't sweat."

✿ ✿ ✿

In 1939, three dollars a week was hardly enough for even a teen-ager to live on. So I decided to get myself hired by CJOR in Vancouver on a regular basis. There was no sense in applying for a job, as there was no such demand. I had to create one.

At 9:00 A.M. I sat in a corner of the waiting room to absorb the atmosphere. When I felt someone was staring at me too long or suspiciously, I left. But I always returned. One morning the newscaster, Richard Diespecker, came out of the studio and shouted for a cup of coffee.

The next morning, when he came out, I had his coffee ready and waiting. The same thing happened the following day, and the next. One day before his broadcast, he came out of his office and handed me some news items which had come over the wire.

"I haven't got time to edit these, kid," he instructed me, as if I had been around for years. "Do me a favor—blacken out the errors, and underline the proper names."

I did so. I also spelled out the difficult foreign names and stapled the bulletins onto stiff cards to make them easier to handle. Within a couple of weeks, I was hired as news preparer, office boy, evening phone-answerer, and *Bathnight Revue* regular—at $15 per week!

Moral: If you stay inconspicuous but become innovative, you will soon be indispensable.

Richard Diespecker was also CJOR's program director and scriptwriter for the station's one-hour dramatic offering, a weekly news-documentary type show, presented by a small cast of actors. I soon became a regular.

In time, I not only typed the scripts, I also helped write them. I was now an actor-writer! Also phone answerer, news assistant, fill-in disc jockey, comedian . . . and, after a few weeks, fired!

The station owner had looked at the schedule of employees and their activities. Deciding that I might soon be asking for a raise, he simply placed a note in my envelope telling me I was "overqualified" and paid me off.

"Look, ma. No beard."

As I walked home, I felt empty. My sister Hattie and I had recently moved to Vancouver and rented a room and kitchen a mile from the station. Now all this luxury had to be surrendered!

My friend's words came back to me: "What happens to you isn't important. It's how you handle it when it happens. That's important!"

There and then I decided that I must have been fired because something new and wonderful was about to happen. Excited, I began to run home. I couldn't wait to tell my sister of the marvelous development in my career.

The optimism of youth was rewarded. Two days later, I got a call from the Canadian Broadcasting Corporation. They were starting a new show called "Stag Party," a sort of men's magazine of the air. Could I write a men's fashion report in a humorous way? And also a light interview with "humorous commentary"?

I wrote the script and sent it to the producer. "I like the writing," he said. "But what have you done to the 'humorous commentary'? It's supposed to be read by just one person."

I answered carefully, "Well, I thought it might become monotonous with an announcer reading for half an hour, so I added some other voices to give him a break."

"But you've got Scottish dialects, cockney voices, and old men. Our announcer chaps can't do that."

The iron was hot. I hit. "Gosh, I didn't think of that. But if you like the material, I'd be glad to do those little extras for the same money," I volunteered.

So, at the age of seventeen, I was writing, performing, and, in a matter of weeks, starring in a national network program. The following month, they changed the title to "The Alan Young Show."

Presenting a comedy show each week was a challenging, but thrilling experience. It was also my first frustrating brush with bureaucracy. Working for the then-government-owned CBC could be a pain in the neck—especially since most of those at the top were retired school principals or other civil-servant types who didn't have a clue about show business.

Many times I arrived at the studio to do my show, only to be told that the bureaucrats had decided to bump it to another night.

The sad thing was that the extremely rare CBC comedy shows— mine was the only one at the time—were generally moved to accommodate more "substantial" network fare: a special string-quartet recital, or poetry readings by our regional director. Absolute fact!

After writing, acting, and directing my show for a year, I felt I was worth more than the $50 a week I was getting.

"What do you propose?" the regional director asked, smiling patronizingly.

"At least $75," I suggested tentatively.

He sighed patiently and shook his head. "Do you realize that if I gave you that much, you'd be paid more than our symphony viola player? And he does two shows."

Finally he agreed to another $25—but for that I had to agree to act in a dramatic series as well.

The first dramatic production I was hired for was the Canadian debut of the British Broadcasting Corporation blockbuster, "Flags on the Matterhorn," a nail-biting account of the conquest of the man-killing peak in the Swiss Alps.

The play had been presented thrillingly by the BBC in England with the full London Philharmonic orchestra, three multi-miked studios, a huge special-effects department, and a cast of thirty.

It was now going to be done in Vancouver. Our twelve-piece band wasn't bad, but we had only seven actors, one studio, and no sound-effects man.

Lance Seivking, our despondent English director, hid his frustration and urged us to improvise.

Each actor carried his own box of cornstarch which, when squeezed, gave off a sort of squeaky crunch, much like footsteps in the snow. A bicycle wheel, rotated at speed close to old window shades, produced an adequate wind effect. All of this, combined with a profusion of "brrs" and chattering teeth, reminded listeners that the Matterhorn was one helluva cold place to be.

The director should have been content. But, like most true artists flushed with success, he went a step further. "I want an echo effect," he said. "Now, I know we don't have an echo chamber, but I was just in the men's washroom, and I have a smashing idea.

"The washroom is all ceramic tile, even the ceiling, and this produces a resounding echo. We'll put in a live microphone—and voila, a true alpine echo!"

It worked brilliantly in dress rehearsal. Shouts from alp to alp were rerouted through our men's room and the illusion was staggering. Our director's eyes were shining with triumphant tears. "The BBC won't know how we did it." he exulted. "We'll be the talk of London!" And we were.

Everything worked perfectly until we went on the air live. Just before our conquering team began the last perilous fifty feet to the peak, our local newscaster, evening paper in hand, paid his usual 8:45 visit to the bathroom. He locked himself in a cubicle, settled down comfortably, and turned noisily to the sports section.

The dramatic climb, as acted out by us shivering, starch-box-squeezing actors, was punctuated by echoed sounds of bathroom preoccupation. With our makeshift wind machine at full blast, the triumphant planting of the flag was drowned out by a more expressive tempest, capped finally by a ten-second flush.

To the listener, it sounded as if half of Switzerland had been washed into the Mediterranean.

Our director returned to England a sadder, wiser and much-less-innovative man.

At that time in Canada, the greatest compliment an entertainer could get was "You know, you're good enough to be in the States." Or worse yet: "You can't be very good or you'd *be* in the States."

Even though I was happy with the show and the country, it seemed as though in Canada hockey players and quintuplets were getting the big money and publicity. So I realized that eventually I'd have to head south.

My opportunity came in a letter from New York theatrical agent, Frank Cooper, whose radio somehow managed to pick up my show from Toronto, some 500 miles away. The accents interested him. Then the laughs attracted him.

I sent Frank a recording of one of my shows. The next I heard, he had sold me as a summer replacement for Eddie Cantor.

Eddie Cantor! The man I had listened to during all my invalid years. Now I was going to get his time spot for my own. Off I went to America—with a return ticket.

6

New York, New York

Adventures in the Big Apple

Mention an immigrant arriving in the United States thirty or forty years ago and you tend to conjure up a picture of a poor, frightened foreigner leaning over the rail of a dirty tramp steamer, oohing and ahing as he spots the Statue of Liberty, right?

Our hearts go out to this lost, innocent soul. We want to help him, guide him. We listen patiently as he asks directions in fractured English. We draw a map for him and send him on his way with a pat and a smile, feeling a deep satisfaction because we have struck a blow for the downtrodden.

But have we ever considered the well-dressed alien who arrives in New York via Canadian Airlines? He speaks English, or so it sounds. Not real English, of course. I mean not English as God and New Yorkers intended it to be spoken.

✿   ✿   ✿

Early radio.

I flew into La Guardia Airport in June 1944, in the middle of the rush hour, which I found lasts twenty-four hours a day. A cab pulled up.

Here I'd like to say how sorry I feel for today's New Yorker who never enjoyed the experience of riding in the taxi of the forties and fifties. Unlike today, the drivers all spoke English—and they spoke a *lot* of it, continuously!

The driver stared at me. I smiled at him. "Are you engaged?" I asked.

What?"

"Are you spoken for?"

Muttering something disparaging about sexual preference he drove off. Another cab took his place. Again the driver sat staring. This time I wasn't about to speak first. I smiled at him, and this evidently broke the ice.

"What is it, buddy?" he asked.

Again I was stuck. If he had said, "Where do you want to go?" or "Please get in," I might have understood. But, "What is it?" I took a wild stab.

"It's Thursday." I volunteered.

He drove off muttering something about smart asses. Finally another cab pulled up and I instantly jumped in,

It was here I discovered another interesting example of New York ingenuity. When the cab door shut, it depressed a button which turned off the interior lights. It also activated another button which started the driver talking.

Of course, it was impossible to understand what he was saying and, as I have since found out, you were not supposed to. He usually had a stubby cigar in his mouth and talked directly into the windshield.

All of this confused helpless visitors. I felt that this man, the first American I had met on this sacred soil was pouring forth words of wisdom, and I was only catching one in ten. I leaned forward as far as possible to listen.

But when he braked suddenly, I cracked my forehead smartly on the meter. When he accelerated, I flipped back and my skull would crunch on the headrest. It was the first conversation I'd ever had that left me with a concussion. I was relieved when we pulled up at the hotel before he had drawn blood.

The Algonquin Hotel in busy Manhattan was a literary intellectual shrine for many years. Its dining room housed the famous "Round Table." Each lunch hour, such New York literary luminaries as Robert Benchley, Charles Butterworth, George S. Kaufman, Dorothy Parker, Franklin P. Adams, and Alexander Woolcott would dine together. Their purpose was not to satisfy their appetites, but verbally to top each other.

Memory, tradition, and gossip have enlarged these gatherings to a table which included everyone from Soupy Sales to the Mormon Tabernacle Choir. But this group was the intellectual nucleus.

1946. I've just arrived in the United States.

In any case, I wasn't staying at the Algonquin. I moved into the Royalton, across the street. Not only did this modest establishment not host a round table, it had no dining facilities whatsoever. But management overlooked cooking in the room.

So I didn't join the Round Table literati, but I did have a brush with their greatness.

My first impression of New York that long, hot summer was that it was a very warm place, oppressively warm. Air conditioning was scarce in those days.

In the Royalton, the only time the air was conditioned was when the house detective belched through the keyhole. (This is an old Fred Allen line I cleaned up.) I managed to maintain some semblance of fresh air by leaving the windows and door wide open. This introduced a slight breeze into the room, as well as unexpected visitors.

One evening I looked up from my reading. It was a book I had found in the nightstand; it had been donated by a delightful man named Gideon. Standing in my doorway were two of the most glamorous, beautiful and disappointed-looking young ladies I had ever seen.

"Are you Mr. Butterworth?" one of the girls asked, looking ravishing, but still disappointed.

"Or maybe you're Mr. Benchley," suggested the other, looking pretty much the same way.

"No." I said, thinking quickly.

"Isn't this Room 308?" asked the brunette, her eyelashes fluttering like a butterfly in heat.

"Yes," I countered cleverly.

"And there's no Mr. Benchley or Mr. Butterworth here?" the blonde asked tremulously, her lips moist, her earlobes trembling. A trembling earlobe drives me mad.

"No," I said, after a weak moment of maddening hesitation.

"Oh, sorry. We must have the wrong room."

And off they went.

This happened on two or three occasions with different young ladies, but always the same scenario. Finally I decided that this should be reported to the desk clerk. After all, this was a fairly reputable third-class hotel, and these occurrences were a little peculiar.

"I've been getting some rather odd visitors in the evening," I said to the young night clerk.

"I know," he smiled, with what I detected as a leer. "How about that?"

"It's young ladies with the wrong room."

"I know, I know." He nodded enthusiastically.

"They are looking for a different room." I persisted. "I'm in 308."

He stopped smiling and spoke very slowly. "What do you tell them?"

"I suggest they try 408 or 508 or 608."

The clerk looked at me as though I were a specimen under glass. "I thought I was doing you a favor," he breathed quietly.

"A favor?"

"Yeah. Every night you go out and have a hamburger, then go up to your room. You look lonely. Every night, the most beautiful broads in the world come here looking for Room 408. And every night I send a couple of them to 308, your room! I figured—share the wealth!" He turned away disgustedly. "It just goes to show you—Communism will never work in America."

I later discovered that Room 408 was kept by literary pundits Robert Benchley and Charles Butterworth for entertaining friends. I always wanted to tell them that I nearly siphoned off some of their gorgeous visitors. But I didn't.

One of the first things I did when I arrived in New York was legally to change my name. My birth certificate says Angus Young, a name I was quite proud of. But it seemed to puzzle New Yorkers. "Angus—that's a cow isn't it?" Or: "Is your name really Agnes?"

Being a twenty-year-old anxious to get ahead, I got fed up with these questions. So Angus became Alan.

I was in total awe of the New York radio milieu. My first time on the air in the Big Apple was a guest spot on a show featuring the great Paul Whiteman and his orchestra; Tallulah Bankhead, who currently was starring in the Alfred Hitchcock movie *Lifeboat;* that wonderful maestro of pantomime Zero Mostel; and veteran actor Walter Huston, who sang his memorable "September Song."

What a show! I remember waiting my turn, sitting in the studio with an elegant lady who was not a performer. And I'm ashamed to admit that I recall thinking she wasn't very pretty.

She said to me, "So you're from Canada. I do hope you're going to like it here in America."

I replied: "Thank you very much, Miss . . . or is it Mrs. . . . ?"

"Just call me Eleanor," she replied graciously. "I have a husband named Franklin."

I figured it out on the way back to my hotel.

Rehearsals for my new radio show were about to get under way; the first broadcast was looming near. But Frank Cooper, the producer-director, and the sponsor, were unhappy about the scripts, and so was I. I'd had more fun with an impacted tooth. We did live test previews, and they were as exciting as listening to a dial tone.

With Polly Bergen. Our first guest star on "The Alan Young TV Show" and her first big break.

I finally got enough nerve one day to question one of the writers. "That second joke didn't get much of a laugh," I ventured.

"Of course not," he answered quickly. "You pronounced a word wrong. You can't get a laugh when you pronounce a word wrong."

"Wrongly," I said.

"What?"

"You don't pronounce something wrong, you pronounce it wrongly."

"That's what I said. It was all wrongly!"

The other writers joined in and pointed out that I had pronounced the word "boss" incorrectly. The correct pronunciation was "bo-ahs."

"But isn't that just 'New Yorky'?" I asked.

"Bo-ahs," they repeated.

Not understanding many of the jokes, as well as being told that my pronunciation was suspect did nothing to raise my confidence and it certainly added to my panic. This became near-hysteria with the sudden realization that my show's opening was only a week away!

✲   ✲   ✲

Ten minutes before airtime, I was standing backstage, waiting to walk out and begin the audience warm-up. As I reached for the curtain, one of the ex-writers walked up to me. "How kind," I thought. "He isn't holding a grudge. Even though he was fired, he's come to wish me well."

Instead, he looked at me coldly and said, "I've just read the new script you're going on the air with. You're gonna lay an egg. Lots of luck." Then he walked away.

With those words of encouragement still ringing in my ears, I stepped onstage to meet my first American audience. Halfway through the warm-up, a man came rushing down the aisle.

The audience cheered and applauded. They obviously knew him, but I didn't recognize him.

"So, you're the Canadian comic," he said. "I predict you have a fine chance to become a big hit . . . a fine chance to become a top comedian . . . a fine chance to go on for years!" He paused for his punch line. "Yeah—a fine chance!"

He left to laughter and applause. I knew the joke and winced when I heard the punch line coming. I love comedians, but I felt that while this guy's timing was good, his sensitivity was missing.

I realized later that Milton Berle didn't intend his interruption to be hurtful. When a new performer came along, he wanted to be there; and when there was an audience, he just couldn't help talking. At least that's the kindest conclusion I could come to.

The show went on, and lived down to its expectations. That night I double-checked to make sure I still had my round-trip ticket to Canada. Oh, how I longed to use it there and then!

We did the show from the old Vanderbilt Theater. The bathroom was about ten feet from the stage entrance. Almost every week for the first two months, just before my entrance, I would rush to the bathroom, throw up, and get back just in time for my introduction.

One night Frank witnessed my panic. He was furious. "From

"Gimme that again. You're going to ride who into what battle?"

now on, don't you ever read the script before you go on the air!" he screamed.

The show must have improved because after my three-month replacement run, the sponsor gave me my own permanent time slot.

I was now free to hire my own writers and cast of regular characters. And there were some brilliant radio performers in New York at that time.

Looking back over the old scripts, I see that I worked with the best. Thelma Ritter, Minerva Pious, Mercedes McCambridge, Art Carney, Jack Albertson, Jack Kirkwood, and Ed Begley were among our impressive stock company.

I couldn't maintain complete autonomy, and lost some of our best characters because the sponsor didn't care for them. Our sponsor lived to regret two of these early casualties.

"A Palomino Pilgrim!"

Our announcer, Kenny Delmar, doubled in the part of a raucous Southern politico, Counselor Cartenbranch, in some of our skits. He had many catchphrases, including "It's a joke, son!"

Top character actor Parker Fennelley played one of my Canadian characters as a crotchety, monosyllabic New Englander. Both actors were sensational, but we were forced to write them out.

A few weeks later, Fred Allen called and asked whether we were ever going to use Kenny or Parker again. When we told him no, Fred immediately hired both for his own show and changed their names to Senator Claghorn and Titus Moody. They became the radio hits of the year.

As a result, we were looking desperately for comedy characters. The writers—by now I had two excellent writers, the late Norman Paul and David R. Schwartz, now retired—and I would listen to actors daily as they paraded before us the wildest voices you can imagine.

One of my favorites was a character Jim Backus developed. He had dreamed up a loud Groton individual who enunciated broad "a's" through clenched teeth. Jim had the incongruous idea of playing this character as a fish peddler. It was hilarious. We began to write the spot but, as it progressed, we could see it was obviously a one-joke bit. We dropped the idea.

I suggested to the writers that a good antagonist for me would be a character who was the direct opposite of mine. I played a poor young man; he should be rich. I was quiet and shy; he should be loud and boastful.

Norman and Dave went off and in two days they came through with one of the funniest characters imaginable. His name was Hubert Updike III, and he confessed modestly to being the richest man in the world. Now to get the right actor to play Hubert.

Arnold Stang, an extremely funny man with a bow tie and receding chin, was cast in the part. But while Arnold was his usual funny self, the voice and character just didn't match. Our test audience loved Arnold, but Hubert Updike didn't come across.

Then I remembered the stuffy Groton accent of Jim Backus's fish peddler. Jim came in, did the part, and Hubert Updike III was born! Within a matter of weeks, Hubert's hilarious "rich" jokes were being repeated by our loyal listeners.

Unfortunately, we were on what was called NBC's Blue Network, later sold off to become the American Broadcasting Company. The Blue Network did not enjoy a large listening audience.

Being on the Blue Network was . . . how can I describe it? It was like living in Pomona. You know there is such a place, but you don't know where it is! Had the show been on a larger network I'm sure Hubert Updike would have been a national treasure.

We had to settle for being all the rage in Helena, Montana, upper Vermont, many sections west of Biloxi, and all the boys at the transmitter.

Even though I had been raised in radio and was making a good living from it, I still wasn't sure whether it was my medium. I realized that I would have to broaden my horizons in the entertainment business, "enlarge my use-abilities," as they say in show biz.

After all, it was the only business I knew, and I wanted to stay in it. The money's good, the hours are short, and there's no heavy lifting.

But you have to be good at more than one thing. As an old vaudevillian once said to me, "Bein' a performer is like bein' a banjo. If ya only got one string, ain't nobody gonna pluck ya."

Having made up my mind that I wanted to go on to do bigger and better things, I began asking my radio audience to stay behind after the show and I would do an additional half-hour routine for them.

I did this for three reasons. First, because I felt the audience deserved more comedy from me than they got from the radio performance. Second, I loved working "in one"—as it was then called—facing live audiences and getting their instant reactions, good or bad. Third, I was particularly fond of doing physical and pantomime gags, which just don't translate to radio.

Doing this little bonus show opened up a Pandora's box for me because our sponsor's ad-agency executives, Lee Bristol and Joe Allen, began staying behind for the "after-show" spot, which they watched from the sponsor's glassed-in box above the audience.

They had not been especially happy that my show was offering more and more situation comedy, instead of the straight laugh show they had brought down from Canada. So I started getting memos from them, asking, "Include that piece from the after show in the radio program. The audience loved it, and so did we!"

Well, doing pantomime on radio proved to be a bit of a problem. Hearing laughs and no voices had our home audiences checking their sets.

But again, I sensed these new problems were not such bad things after all. They were merely omens of bigger and better developments in the future.

Around this time, the writers had written a gag in the show using Hollywood producer Darryl F. Zanuck's name somewhat in vain. At the time, I hadn't a clue who he was, but I was soon to find out.

We received a letter from 20th Century Fox Studio's legal department, saying it was considering a million dollar lawsuit over the unauthorized use of its president's name. Now I knew who Darryl F. Zanuck was!

The following week, I apologized and gave a nice plug for one of Fox's upcoming movies, and all was forgiven. This somehow gave my manager some kind of backdoor entry into the Fox studio in New York. In the fall of 1945, I reported for a screen test at Fox's Tenth Avenue studios in New York City.

A man shoved me in front of a camera and told me to tell my jokes. I did all my surefire material. I bounced, I grinned, I leered. I gave them every expression and nuance I ever heard or imagined. Oh, I gave them a screen test all right.

A few days later, the talent scout asked if I'd like to see the test before it was sent to Zanuck. Did I ever! I'd never seen myself on film.

The lights went out in the projection room, the test appeared on the screen, and slowly the hot air began to seep out of my head. Right before my eyes, a wild-eyed, frenetic young man sprang into view in what is called a "close head-shot."

My face filled the twenty-foot screen. When I moved, half my head disappeared. When I grinned, the sides of my mouth shot out the sides of the picture. I raised my eyebrows, and they scooted up and over the top. Eyes and teeth were flashing all over the wall. It was like watching a Ping-Pong ball in a blender.

The test finished, the lights went on, and I crawled out from under the seats, looking for the security of the nearest radio. "Different, isn't it?" The talent scout, a cherubic-faced young man named Meyer Mishkin, smiled kindly.

Then he introduced me to a kind-looking man who had also

California. You just gotta
love it.

witnessed my debacle. It's comforting to meet kind-looking men
when you have just bombed.

The older gentleman's last name was Simon, and he had worked
for the great theatrical impresario, David Belasco. Mr. Simon gently raised the problems with my test by explaining how theatrical
movements just do not fit a camera lens.

"Subtlety and the inner spark are demanded," he told me. "It's
je ne sais quoi,' and if you haven't got it, nothing will make up
for it."

He said if I wrote a little sketch, showing what I really could do,
he would direct it for me. The next day I wrote a five-minute scene
about a shy young man coming to call on a girl. He is insulted by
the girl's father, who considers him a total zero. In the ensuing
conversation, the young man gently outwits the father and leaves
with the delighted girl. Simple scene.

As a favor to me, the late great Ed Begley, who went on to become an Oscar winner, played the father.

In fact this test turned out to be both our passports to Hollywood.

7

Hooray for Hollywood

My train pulled into Pasadena on January 6, 1946. I took one look at California, and that same day cashed in my return ticket to Canada.

Nothing personal. I love Britain and Canada, but I had found my home.

I moved into a room in the Hollywood Plaza Hotel. The Plaza was then at the hub of Hollywood's radio world—across from the Brown Derby, a block north of NBC and two blocks east of CBS. George Burns had his office on the top floor, and Errol Flynn had his in the bar.

At Fox, the big picture on the shooting schedule was an epic called *Forever Amber*. It had been shooting for months with a famous imported cast.

Suddenly, with a crack of Zanuck's riding crop, the shooting stopped. Thousands of film feet were scrapped, actors paid off, more tests, and they started back at "letter A" with new everybody.

Amber still flopped. It cost Fox a fortune. As it turned out, my first picture, a little four-month opus called *Margie,* regained all the money *Amber* lost.

I went on salary at $2,000 per week, a figure that boggled my mind. Naturally, I kept reporting to the studio for work every morning until the casting director, that great silent star Ben Lyon, took me aside.

"You don't have to come in here every day," Ben said kindly. "You come only when we give you what is called a 'cast call.' "

"But I feel guilty getting paid for doing nothing," I protested.

"Then give the money back," he laughed.

That guilty I didn't feel. A week or so later I, received a call from a second assistant director, a young man called Howard Koch, who is now one of the industry's most successful independent producers. He is also one of the nicest men I have ever met.

"You go to work at two o'clock tomorrow," Howard told me.

"Great," I responded eagerly. "Where's the script? What do I do? Where's the makeup department?"

"Hold it! You won't be shooting," Howard explained patiently. "You have to report to the Sonja Henie Ice Palace in Westwood. Every day you'll have a two-hour skating lesson. You see, there's going to be an ice-rink scene in your picture."

This conversation was unbelievable. In Canada boys were put on ice right after the christening. They were slid to the baptism, and had to skate home after the circumcision. They were going to pay me for skating lessons?

"Howard," I said. "It isn't right that I get paid $2,000 a week for taking skating lessons"

"You want to give the money back?"

No way. I had learned. For a month, I took skating lessons in the afternoon and learned how to drive a model-T Ford in the morning.

With my newfound wealth, I persuaded my mother and father to leave drafty Vancouver and join me in California. Soon we were comfortably ensconced in a new home in the San Fernando Valley.

Margie was shot and released quickly. It was an instant hit. It generated a rebirth of dances and songs of the 1920s. "Sweet Sue" and the charleston became as familiar in 1946 as wedgies.

Now, with my first picture a hit, I had nothing to do for the rest of the summer but wait for the next picture to come along.

In the 1940s, NBC sponsored the annual Christmas parade down Hollywood Boulevard. Every star of an NBC show had the privilege of entering a float in the procession. It was tremendous publicity.

As I needed all the promotion I could get, the "Alan Young Radio Show" was represented. Ben Lyon promised to send over some of Fox's starlets to grace my float. I figured that very few people would recognize me—but they would certainly pay attention to a bevy of beautiful young ladies.

After the parade, we all retired to the Brown Derby, some to drink, but for us young nondrinkers, just to have food.

One of the actresses from my float was very shy and quiet. I was also shy, so we found each other sitting together. Her name was Norma Jean Dougherty, and we sat side by side silently.

Conrad Janis, an actor in our picture *Margie*, had invited me to his house for a party the following night. I had no date, so I decided to take a chance with this wide-eyed eighteen-year-old.

"Would you like to go to a party with me tomorrow?" I asked.

She hesitated, then said unenthusiastically, "Okay."

She said she lived with her grandmother and gave me an address in Santa Monica. The following evening I knocked on the door and it was opened by an attractive white-haired lady, who introduced herself as Ana Lower, and welcomed me in. She said Norma would be out in a minute. Would I care to sit down?

As we chatted, I could tell that she was sizing me up trying to ascertain what kind of man was taking her little girl out. Suddenly I spotted a familiar picture on the wall. "Isn't that the Mother Church in Boston?" I said.

She immediately brightened. "How did you know?"

I told her I had attended Christian Science Sunday school. From then on, our conversation flowed freely. I later learned that Ana

With Bill Thompson and
Marilyn Monroe.

was not Norma Jean's grandmother, but a loving lady who had been taking care of her for the past eight years.

Little Norma had bounced from orphanages to foster homes for most of her existence and, at the age of twelve, Ana took her in for what proved to be the longest and happiest home life the little girl had ever experienced.

In a few minutes, Norma appeared. She was wearing a skirt and sweater, both of which she filled out perfectly. She must have overheard part of my conversation with Ana, because as we drove east toward the San Fernando Valley I could hardly get a word in edgewise as she enthused about her experiences with Ana, who was a Christian Science practitioner, how much she enjoyed going to Sunday school, and on and on.

In those days, the hills separating Hollywood from the valley were often enveloped in dense fog, and this was one of those foggy evenings.

As I drove through Coldwater Canyon, I could barely see the

road. I realized I would never find Conrad's house without explicit directions. My home was close to the canyon, so I drove there instead. As I pulled up in my driveway, Norma asked quietly, "Is this Conrad's house?"

"No," I said. "It's mine. You see, this way I can phone him and get precise directions."

Norma pulled back in her seat. I could see she didn't believe a word of it. Here was another man trying to take advantage of her.

"Come on in," I said. "You can't sit out here in the fog. Besides, I live with my mother and father."

This reassured her slightly, so in she came. However, my parents were anything but reassured when they saw me walk in with this beautiful blonde in the well-filled skirt and sweater.

In the Old Country, when you bring a girl home to meet your parents, it generally means your intentions are somewhat serious. Mom and Dad had just arrived in America, and the fast pace of Hollywood was a little staggering.

"Norma Jean was telling me about going to our Sunday school," I said to break the ice.

"How nice," replied my father, looking her square in the sweater.

Mother had hurried to put the kettle on. It was an old British tradition: when confused or in doubt, have a cup of tea! I made my call to Conrad, got the directions, and rushed Norma Jean back to the car.

I don't remember much about the party, but I got the feeling that Norma Jean seemed ill at ease around groups of strangers. And, oddly, she didn't seem to relate comfortably to people her own age.

When I drove her home early and walked her to the door, there was one of those awkward pauses where you wonder whether she'll think you're square if you shake hands, or pushy if you kiss her.

I opted for a gentle portion of the latter. As I got my face closer to hers, she offered me her cheek gently. I kissed it, thanked her, and took off.

Six years later, I was sitting in a makeup chair in the RKO studios when a glamorous blonde beauty walked in.

"Alan," she said delightedly. "How are you?"

"Fine," I replied. "How are you?"

I wanted to say "Who are you?" because I hadn't a clue who she was. We spoke for a few moments in generalities. Then she kissed me on the cheek and took off. My makeup man was impressed. "Wow, you're a friend of Marilyn Monroe's?" he said admiringly.

Now I remembered. On a neighboring sound stage, Marilyn-Norma was shooting *Clash by Night*—a movie that would take her out of fourth or fifth billing and turn her into the world's hottest movie star. I never met her again.

But I've never forgotten Norma Jean, a little girl who loved her Sunday school.

Another popular Hollywood event in the 1940s was the annual baseball game at Gilmore Field called "Comedians versus Leading Men."

Pretty actresses, dressed in shorts and T-shirts, made up the cheering section as cheerleaders, bat girls, assistant trainers, or whatever. It was an event well covered by the news media and photographed by all the movie-fan magazines.

In 1947 I was invited to be a member of the comedians' team. Being of British origin, I wasn't particularly good at baseball. Though the game was played in Canada, I had leaned more to soccer and hockey.

However, it was explained to me that while the leading men were expected to play well, the comedians' main job was to get laughs. For my bit of shtick, I decided that I would pretend to get hit with a ball. Then my two writers would rush out with a stretcher. With me on it, they would then run the bases, sliding into the plate for a home run, stretcher and all.

Since I still wasn't too familiar with Los Angeles, by the time I arrived at the field, the game had started. The leading men were at bat as I ran toward the field with my stretcher under my arm.

Just as I stepped out of the tunnel, a man grabbed the stretcher from me, yelling, "Good thinking, fella!" and rushed out onto the field. My comedy routine was totally sabotaged before I even got started!

Apparently, a leading man named Ronald Reagan had been at bat, hit a line drive, and raced to first base. George Tobias, a large, strong comedian caught the throw, but collided accidentally with Reagan, sending him flying.

As he turned to apologize, he heard a loud clicking sound. "Don't click your tongue at me, Ron," quipped the comedian. "It was an accident."

"That isn't my tongue clicking, George. It's my leg. I think it's broken!"

They placed our future president gently on my stretcher and carried him off. Doctors later found it to be a serious series of breaks which almost left him crippled.

Meanwhile, there I stood on the field, empty-handed and gag-less.

"You're on next," the comedians' coach told me. "What's your comedy bit?"

"There isn't one," I said. "My gag is carrying Ronald Reagan to the hospital."

So began and ended my baseball career!

I felt privileged to be part of the remaining halcyon days of Hollywood.

Hollywood was far from the den of iniquity many outsiders made it out to be. Actors then were like one big happy family. Okay, there were feuds and infighting, and some actors chose not to speak to others. But all in all, we still were part of the same family.

There was a clubby feeling about living and working in Hollywood. For example, Oscar night was a dinner back then. You didn't go to the Academy Awards, you went to the Academy Awards dinner.

And you could enjoy a stroll down Sunset Boulevard any evening

"At the Patsy Awards. That's Lester, me, Wilbur, Bud Weatherwax, a dog, and Jay North (Dennis the Menace). I hate it when photographers catch you with your tongue out."

and expect to bump into one or two stars out window shopping. Today you walk down Sunset at night alone—and you can expect to see stars, all right!

Saturday nights were when everyone went nightclubbing. And Ciro's was a favorite haunt for dinner and dancing—if you didn't happen to be working, which happened a lot back then.

At Ciro's, all the stars got ringside tables around the dance floor. We young upstarts were seated against the back walls.

But we didn't mind. It was a great vantage point for star-struck up-and-comers to watch our movie idols at play. Seated at his usual ringside table was Ciro regular Herbert Marshall. Even though I learned he had an artificial leg, he was one heckuva dancer.

On Saturday evening I had the good fortune to bump into Merle Oberon, one of my idols, on the dance floor. My tongue stuck to the roof of my mouth when I came face to face with one of the most beautiful faces in the world.

And Miss Oberon recognized me! "You are a funny young man," she told me huskily.

I was frozen to the spot. "Huh?" I ad-libbed wittily.

"You are a funny young man," she repeated, flashing me a heart-melting smile.

I didn't know what to say. I struggled with my tongue, fighting for the right words. "Same to you!" I blurted finally.

One night at Ciro's is still etched graphically in my memory. Everyone's eyes turned to the main entrance as a majestic figure entered and stood at the top of the entrance stairs, surveying the action.

It was an Arabian sheik, dressed resplendently in magnificent robes. With him was an entourage of beautiful girls, along with several obligatory bodyguards.

The sheik was carrying a chamois bag. He undid a cord, reached into the bag, and produced a beautiful gem which he handed to the maître d'.

With that he was ushered to the largest and best table in the

"Wilbur is sitting on a $50,000 silver saddle. I'm wearing my new nonslip leather shoes, triple-triple E."

room. Busboys and waiters were tripping over each other to fulfill the group's every desire.

They weren't disappointed. When he was seated, he reached into the chamois pouch again and handed each of the eager staff a beautiful gem.

Well, for the next hour or so every eye in the room was on the sheik's party. He didn't dance, but we watched in fascination as he sat at his table, nuzzling each of his beautiful girl companions in turn. Every now and then, he opened his bag and presented a girl with a gem.

Finally they were ready to leave. The bill came. He opened his bag and paid for it his usual lavish way.

Everyone froze as he tripped while walking to the door. The room was hushed. His guards grabbed him, so he didn't fall, but his chamois bag of goodies fell out of his hands.

It burst open as it hit the floor—and diamonds, rubies, emeralds, large and small, went flying everywhere.

The sheik regained his composure, surveyed the precious stones strewn over the floor, and gave a contemptuous "Ech!" Then he and his entourage walked out.

For a few seconds, there was silence. Then pandemonium broke out. Stars, semi-stars, and star watchers began falling over themselves as they dived to grab a gem!

It wasn't until the next morning's newspapers I learned that our sheik had really been an enterprising press agent named Jim Moran who was publicizing the release of the movie *Ali Baba.*

His girls and bodyguards were from Central Casting. And his precious baubles were from Woolworth's.

He certainly got his publicity.

My first summer in Hollywood was almost over, and I hadn't been offered another picture. I was disappointed. I had felt confident that after the success of *Margie*, I would be flooded with offers.

But things just weren't happening for me. I soon found out the disturbing reason for this inactivity.

Under the studio system back then, producers could put a "hold" on a contract player if they had something in mind for him. That way none of the other producers could use the actor in their films until further notice.

I was one of those actors on hold. In my case, at the Fox studio, Walter Morosco, the producer of *Margie*, said he wanted me for his next picture. Apparently, he had great faith in me and intended giving me the big buildup.

Some excellent script ideas came my way, and I loved them. I was puzzled when, one after another, they were postponed, shelved, and subsequently dropped.

Only later I learned the reason: Morosco had become very ill, incapacitated for several months. Within a year, he died.

It seemed my opportunities had come and gone. By the time I found out, the other producers had their pictures on the drawing board, and I was scheduled for nothing.

I was and still am quite philosophical about the way things

turned out. That's the way of our business. And I was always grateful for Walter Morosco's interest and faith in me.

By the spring of 1947, the entire motion-picture business was experiencing a radical change. In December 1946, *Variety* sounded the death knell for the golden days of Hollywood when it reported: "The era of wonderful nonsense is over. The past year was, and henceforth will go down as the awakening."

The awakening was a rude one. Hollywood found itself at the end of its bonanza years. I was grateful to have experienced at least a year of the extravagant days . . . a time of studios maintaining stables of highly paid contract actors, writers, and directors.

The *Film Daily Year Book* reported a total of 804 actors, 490 writers, and 152 directors under contract to major studios when I arrived in Hollywood. The following year that number was cut in half.

This turn of events was perfectly understandable. Those so-called golden years were a period when time and money meant very little. Extravagance and waste was the order of the day.

These were days when nubile young starlets were hired not so much for their promise, but their promises. Sometimes it took a six-month shooting schedule just to film a movie's credits.

Sad, but true. Many fine young actors fell by the wayside. I still could fall back on what had always been my prime source of employment: radio.

8

Changing Gears

The year 1948 was my last in radio. It was also my best financially—but I had to star in two shows to do it.

Besides having my own show on Sunday evenings, I played Jimmy Durante's sidekick on Friday nights.

Jimmy hired me hoping I'd be a strong straight man, relieving him of some of the pressure involved in sustaining a show all by himself.

He encouraged me to make him his whipping boy. "Push me around, Youngie," he urged me. "Hit me. I can't get mad unless youse hit me!"

Unfortunately, our partnership never really clicked. You see, I played the same gentle character that Jimmy did. And when I tried to play the tough straight-man routine, I had all the menace of a rabid caterpillar.

We worked at it, but it just wasn't meant to be. It was too late to start changing the character I had established on radio. In any case, the show had run its course and was headed for cancellation in a few months' time. Television was rearing its beautiful head.

But working with Jimmy Durante for that brief period was worth the experience, regardless of these unfortunate circumstances. He was a gem. I saw him angry, frustrated, disappointed, and hurt—but never cruel, thoughtless, or unkind.

During one tense rehearsal, Jimmy was under pressure and told me off rather harshly. I was a trifle steamed, but I couldn't bring myself to answer him back—because I loved him. And, as the star, he was carrying a heavy load. Besides, I probably deserved it.

During our meal break, I could tell Jimmy felt remorseful. He was having a glass of water and a burned bun—he had stomach trouble and the doctor prescribed dry, almost-charcoal-toasted bread as part of his diet.

I sat beside him, feeling sorry for myself. I wasn't eating. I didn't feel the least bit hungry. Jimmy lifted his head a little and squinted at me. Finally, he tore his charred bun in half and held it out. "Here, Youngie," he said. "Youse gotta eat something."

That was Jimmy Durante. No matter how much or how little he had, he shared.

A more exhilarating memory came on one of our last shows together, when the great Al Jolson was Jimmy's guest star.

When the show went off the air and the audience began filing out of the studio, the irrepressible Jolson ran impulsively out onstage.

"Just a minute, folks!" he shouted in inimitable Jolson style. "You ain't heard nothin' yet!"

Then he proceeded to entertain the delighted audience for about half an hour. I sat with Jimmy in the control room, entranced by this great entertainer.

Jimmy was more starry-eyed than anyone. Finally, as Jolson was finishing his impromptu encore, he turned to us with tears in his eyes. "Fellas," he said softly, "wotta privilege. Youse is lookin' at a 'erra'!"

This humble little man didn't realize that we all considered him an equally great part of the same "erra."

After three months, I was dropped from the Durante show. It was the first time I'd been fired since CJOR in Vancouver. Six months later, my own show was dropped by the sponsor.

But I didn't sit around licking my wounds. As before, I just knew that something better was in store for me.

Awaiting my television opportunity, I took to the road, on what was known then as the "stage-show circuit." There were eight or nine theaters in the country which still had strong roots in vaudeville. They put on a ninety-minute variety show, followed by a first-run movie.

It was a grind, but it paid well.

You were expected to do five shows a day, which wasn't bad if you just sang or played the kazoo. But my exuberant act consisted of a monologue, a song, and a bagpipe solo. It was the most strenuous workout I'd had in years.

I opened at the Chicago Theater. The first-run movie was the runaway hit *Going My Way*, starring Bing Crosby and Barry Fitzgerald, and the stage show was the "New Acts Revue," starring Alan Young, Walter Liberace (as he was then called), the Lind Brothers, and our opening dance act, Tommy and Jeanne Mahoney.

Our show opened on Monday, and the headliner—in this case, me—lived on a diet of fingernails until Wednesday's *Variety*. If the box-office grosses were high enough, you enjoyed a long, healthy run. If not, you could expect to be dispatched to some anonymous theater in Lubbock, Texas.

I couldn't wait to get my hands on *Variety* to see how its critics received us. The paper's August 31, 1949, issue headlined under "Picture Grosses": "*Jolson* Sings Sensational $49,000, Chi: (Chicago) . . . 'Alan Young—Stage Great 70G.'

The paper's review of the "New Acts Revue" was glowing. I can't resist sharing this snippet from it with you:

From walk-on, where he pitches some fast quips, to the end, Young has the audience chuckling.

There's a hilarious bit in which he mangles a specialty song. Then, donning kilts, he plays the Scottish bagpipes. Brought back, he does a nervous youth's first public recitation about a horse, mixing up the various parts of the animal to loud guffaws from the audience.

Ours was a youthful show of then-comparative unknowns. Piano maestro Liberace gave his usual smash performance.

Our show, together with the hit movie, was a tremendous moneymaker. No sooner than were we pronounced a hit, I learned how the theater management could squeeze the goose into laying an extra golden egg.

By carefully cutting out sections of the movie, then starting an hour earlier in the morning and ending an hour later in the evening, they could put on seven shows a day instead of the customary five!

While this was a feather in the cap of us performers, it was also a quill up the other end. Joking, singing, and blowing out your lower colon on the bagpipe is bad enough before morning coffee.

But doing it every three hours until 2:00 A.M., then starting the whole thing over again after an 8:30 A.M. wakeup call, and you realize why Abe Lincoln was so hot on emancipation. I guess it was the greatest training in the world—if you were practicing to be an Iranian hostage.

Our next booking was easier. Liberace and I moved on to the Fox Theater in Detroit, whose headliner was the legendary Louis Armstrong, and I learned how an act could be destroyed. After our last Detroit show, some of us decided to relax together at a local nightclub. The floor show was a comic who proceeded to do my entire routine, word for word!

Our table was stunned. I wanted to climb on the stage and hit him with my bagpipes, but the whole thing seemed like a bad dream.

As if this wasn't enough, after his final applause, he sidled over to our table, looked at me, and asked, "Did I get it right?"

Liberace assured me, "Don't worry. He's a nothing comic. He'll never play any important places. Besides, he was so shocked to see you here, he'll never do your stuff again."

And he didn't—until he got to New York!

I was booked into the Strand Theater, my first appearance on Broadway. After the band rehearsals, a worried theater manager came to me. "You can't do that act," he said. "The comic last week did all that material."

It was the thief from the club in Detroit. I explained to the manager that I had paid $10,000 for this act and it was all I had. "You hired a crook last week," I spluttered.

"Crook, schmook," he said. "He did the act first."

"I wish I could do something else, but this is my whole routine.

"You either know how to
fish or you don't."

Do you want me to just stand there and smile at the people?"

"I wouldn't worry," he said sadly. "There might not be that many people to smile at."

And he was right. It was the first time I ever really bombed. As the old saying goes, "Three seats got up and walked out."

At any other time, this withering reception might have destroyed me. But I was so elated about future plans that it hurt only for twelve hours or so.

Just before opening at the Strand, I had flown to Hollywood to make a pilot for that fast-growing new medium, television.

It was quite a coup. At that time most television shows emanated from New York. Milton Berle was the hottest ticket in the country.

Hollywood had only the Ed Wynn show. And CBS Hollywood was anxious to launch other West Coast productions, or it would lose out to New York completely.

It's probably unfair to suggest that CBS had little confidence in my new show, but the budget speaks for itself. Our opening dance number was allotted $12.50: the cost of renting two ladders and a 2 × 12 wooden board. The four dancers wore their own tennis shorts.

Ed Wynn's show was also on CBS Hollywood—the first comedy show written specifically for the new medium. All the other comedy shows on the tube were primarily televised vaudeville.

While perhaps not the funniest man in the world, Ed Wynn certainly had to be one of the greatest innovators in American theater and radio. He approached television the same way. And was generous with his advice and encouragement.

Writers Dave Schwartz, Leo Solomon, and I would sit for hours with Ed listening to him expound, drinking in his words of wisdom.

"The audience is not coming to the theater," he told us. "We are going to them in their homes. We must be gentler yet funnier, because they have many distractions."

Ed had strong views on the effects of visual comedy over the spoken word. I agreed. I had always loved pantomime. In radio, most of my laughs had come from the studio audience's reaction to my facial expressions.

As expected, Ed Wynn's show cleaned up at the Emmy awards that year. I sent him a congratulatory note, and he responded, "Next year it will be yours."

(It was. My show received two Emmys and also a now-defunct New York award, sponsored by Ed Sullivan, called the "Michael.")

Ed Wynn was the pioneer who explored all the possibilities of this medium in its infancy. It's sad that most chroniclers seem to have overlooked his contributions completely.

Looking back at some of my first live shows in 1950, I cannot believe that these were television's golden days. We could be downright amateurish at times.

Ad-libs had to be added to cover the long pauses between sketch exits and entrances as I hurriedly buttoned the last button and zipped the last zipper. A few times, when I was rushed, I skipped the zipper—and then had to do a whole sketch turning sideways to the camera.

Once the show went on the air, it was on—nonstop, live, viewed right there and then by millions. If you forgot a line, you had to ad-lib something appropriate and hopefully funny. If a prop didn't work, you had to be ready to innovate and create. And pray that you were being funny.

Recently I heard one of TV's pioneers raving about "those good old days." Frankly, I'll take today. It's good to learn by experience, but let the rattlesnake bite somebody else.

Writing three sketches a week wasn't too bad that first year. But the second season became a nerve-racking challenge. In each skit I played a different character.

In one, I portrayed a man taking his first airplane flight. In another, a bumbling plumber's assistant. Then a father expecting his first child. And so on. Two hundred skits a season, each on a different topic, with me doing the lion's share of the performing.

I was getting tired of looking at myself, and I knew the audience would be joining me soon.

Fortunately, a new director, Alan Dinehart, took over the show midway through our second season and came up with a refreshing solution. "What we need to do is take some of the load off you," Alan told me. "We'll get some recognizable stars to work with you in the sketches."

"With our budget?" I said. "Alan, you must be dreaming!" He was. But he made these dreams come true.

The very next show we had Nelson Eddy playing a pirate captain who sang "Shortnin' Bread"! Ward Bond did a wagon-train sketch with me. Cesar Romero made frequent guest appearances, as did some of Hollywood's most celebrated character actors, among them James Gleason, Alan Mowbray, and Wallace Ford. Billie Burke, that Good Witch of the North, also put in an appearance—and brought Toto along!

William Frawley was one of our regular guest performers until he left for a permanent job—as Desi Arnaz's neighbor and best buddy Fred Mertz in "I Love Lucy."

Then, just before *From Here to Eternity* halted his slump and shot him to megastardom, Frank Sinatra allowed me to turn one of his trademark song numbers into a comic catastrophe, then had a romp doing a sketch with me.

"How do you do it?" I asked Alan Dinehart. "Do you have something on these people?"

He laughed. "It never hurts to ask. I know actors. They were all watching your show. They were dying to try television—but nobody had ever asked them before!"

Long before "Mister Ed," my show used animals a great deal, which gave our show a different look. It also gave our soundstage a different color—and smell.

When you're doing a live show with animals, you have to be ready for the unexpected. And when an animal is nervous, you can expect a lot.

In one show, I played the part of an inept wild-animal trainer. I made my entrance on a camel and dismounted. My assistant, a wheezing English bulldog, ran out with my whip and whistle. And the act began.

Out came a baby elephant which stood up on its front legs. Then I brought out a black panther on a leash. It proceeded to walk around me until the leash was wound tightly around my legs. Neither of us was able to move. The panther then looked up at me and snarled. As I bent over to pat the snarling cat, a huge Bengal tiger walked out and locked his jaws around my derriére.

This was the basic sketch as it was conceived and rehearsed.

There was nothing dangerous about all this. The tiger was blind and had a habit of closing his teeth on his trainer's wallet, which he carried in his back pocket. This way the gentle, sightless beast could be led anywhere contentedly.

It was a very safe, simple procedure, as well as a rather pathetic picture. But, viewed from the audience, it looked spectacular.

"The Jail Sketch."

From the CBS press release: "Alan Young, CBS television comic, explains some of the trade tricks used by television artists. Rather than memorize his lines, Young jots them down on pocket linings, shirt sleeves... 'or just any place that's handy', declares Young."

"The Other Man," with Cesar Romero.

Hey, the cameras were scary back then.

With Kay Star: there was no time to change on a live show , you see.

From the CBS press release: "Alan Young warms his scottish father's heart every time he displays his newly-won mastery of the bagpipes. Giving a lilt to the kilt is just one of the zany situations Alan Young finds himself in... when Kroger brings the 'Alan Young Show' to televiewers."

The Optometrist.

"The Shoe Salesman."

"Frank and Jesse James"

Dress rehearsals went over well. The camel was bad-tempered, but obedient. The bulldog wheezed in and out on cue throughout the act. The elephant stood on her head. The panther trussed me with the leash and, when I bent over, I felt the Bengal tiger's huge jaws close on my wallet.

"What a show!" we all chorused.

Of course, in rehearsal, various trainers and owners were hovering around hissing instructions. This wasn't possible on the actual live show, but we convinced ourselves that the animals would perform by habit.

We forgot that animals have other habits more deeply ingrained than stage routines. We also overlooked the fact that there would be unrehearsed reactions from 500 people in the audience.

And then it was show time. The sketch began. I rode in on the camel. The audience gasped and applauded. The camel saw the audience, gasped, and flooded the stage.

The bulldog ran out, slipped in the mess, dropped the whip, swallowed the whistle, and rushed into the wings where he remained for the rest of the sketch, wheezing and whistling.

I grabbed the panther's leash, but he refused to circle me or come anywhere near me. Instead, he circled the camera, climbed the curtain, sprayed the boom man, and climbed down.

The elephant jumped her cue and entered early. Instead of standing on her front legs, she decided to stand on one of mine. I yelled, the panther climbed back up the curtain, and the audience roared.

This frightened the little elephant to the pit of her stomach— her bowels, to be exact. And she let loose, too. Our stage looked as though Noah's ark had made a pit stop.

Only the tiger entered on cue. As far as he was concerned, things were going beautifully. Unfortunately, I still had a grip on the panther's leash. He ran offstage with me in tow, heading up the aisle.

The poor blind tiger, jaws agape, was fumbling for my rear end and the wallet. He came up behind one of the cameramen who was hunched over, looking into his viewer.

"Any port in a storm!" the tiger thought, and he latched on. The cameraman took off, with a triumphant tiger holding fast behind him. Our director closed the curtain, cued the orchestra, and left— presumably for the real-estate business.

While these experiences are great for autobiographies, they were killers when they happened.

This type of live television comedy was just too unpredictable to be successful. I knew there had to be a better way. So did more experienced comedians. I had noticed Jack Benny, George Burns, Desi Arnaz, and others watching our rehearsals from time to time. I knew these pros weren't watching me to learn comedy.

They were learning from my mistakes and analyzing the hazards of live television. Their solution was obvious: put it on film.

Desi was first. Al Simon, a brilliant producer and dear friend who was with me on "Mister Ed," came up with a three-camera film technique.

It was the start of a new era in television comedy. This happened, incidentally, after Lucy and Desi's first pilot had been performed live. That show was declared a disaster by one CBS executive, who also said, "She's great, but we've got to get rid of the husband who can't speak English!"

Meanwhile, George Burns and I jostled over who would get to use the main, best-equipped soundstage. I was there first, but George's show always won out, though I'm sure he never knew of the altercation. His show was new and great. Mine was established, but shaky. He was an accepted star; I was a sparking punk.

This situation precipitated my next decision. It was an unfortunate one, I guess, but at least it was decisive. On the advice of my agents, I said, "Either I go on film or I go off TV."

It wasn't entirely a hasty ultimatum on my part. Losing the show wouldn't turn out to be a financial tragedy for me; I had just signed with Paramount pictures.

Some of my co-stars were human, too.

Anyway, CBS turned down my demands, but made a counter-proposal. Would I move to New York and do the show from there permanently? They had an excellent time spot, the slot following a top new show.

I declined and departed television to follow my reborn movie career.

CBS took my head writer, Leo Solomon, and sent him to New

York to create a new show for a new comedian. The comedian's name was Red Buttons. The show they put on after him was "I Love Lucy."

You win a few, you lose a few.

9

The Movies Revisited

Who the Hell Is Aaron Slick?

Not very often do you get a second chance in life. Now that I was up and running in the movie business for the second time, I was determined to make the most of it.

After all, I didn't exactly set the world on fire my last turn out at 20th Century Fox. Of the three pictures I worked on there, *Margie* was a mild hit, but my other two, *Chicken Every Sunday* and *Mr. Belvedere Goes to College,* were turkeys.

My first motion-picture bow had all the impact of dandruff hitting a wet towel.

But now I was better known and would receive top billing. The game plan at Paramount, where I was to be working, was for a script to be written for me based on the type of comedy I had been doing successfully on television.

They called me their "new Charlie Ray," which meant nothing to me—I had never heard of him. Anyway, they said it enthusiastically so I laughed and said things like "Oh, boy, you're kidding!"

My agent Herman Citron of MCA called me excitedly one day.

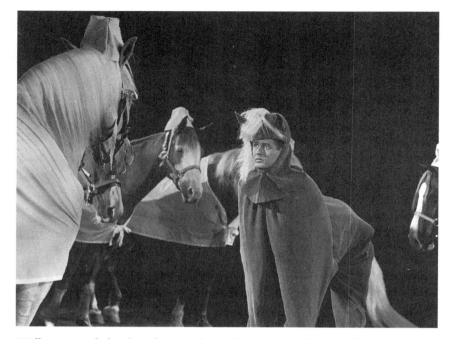

"Wilbur pretended to be a horse so he could join our Lodge. We liked him but couldn't stand his thick thighs."

"They have a picture for you, and it's a natural." Somehow that phrase—"it's a natural"—sounded a warning bell in my head.

The "natural" was called *Aaron Slick from Punkin' Crick*. Again a warning bell sounded in my head—but not loud enough.

In any case, I went through the motions and read the script. It was interesting, but dull. I told my agent that I'd rather pass on this one. The bucolic character of Aaron Slick was too far removed for an ex-British-Canadian whose real name was Angus.

My refusal was met with stony silence. I was asked to attend a meeting at the office of the head of Paramount, Y. Frank Freeman.

Mr. Freeman was a delightful, conservative Southern gentleman who put you at your ease immediately by suggesting that you call him Mr. Freeman. *Aaron Slick* was his baby; he had been trying to get the movie made for years.

"But I just couldn't find the right Aaron," he said. "Now you are the only one who can do this, Aaron."

"Alan," I corrected. "But Mr. Freeman, I just don't understand the story."

"Alan," he smiled. "Have you ever heard of Robbie Burns?"

My Scottish blood tingled. "Has a duck got feathers? Is the Pope Catholic?"

"Don't change the subject. Have you heard of Robbie Burns?"

"Our national hero. Bigger than Johnnie Walker."

"And in Canada, did you know the 'Little Baptiste' stories?"

"What Canadian doesn't?" I enthused.

"Well, Aaron Slick is just as well known in America. Every schoolchild was raised with Aaron Slick adventures, like the Bobbsey Twins and Nancy Drew. The stage play of Aaron was performed more than *Uncle Tom's Cabin!*" (This statement could well have been true—but, if so, it never got performed north of Chattahoochee or west of Hoodoo, Tennessee. In my life, I've met only ten people who ever heard of Aaron Slick, and none who has seen the play!)

"Trust us," Y. Frank Freeman concluded. "We know the business."

My agent joined the friendly persuasion. "Do this for Mr. Freeman, and the second picture will be everything you've dreamed of—at $75,000!"

I agreed.

Later I discovered the whole story. *Aaron Slick* was Freeman's baby. His obsession with that turkey was the joke of the lot. Every new producer was offered it, and everyone turned it down.

I found out later that the latest producing team—whom I knew from their days at Fox—also felt sure the picture would flop, but they figured that they could use it as a wedge to achieve bigger things.

And they had set their sights on Dinah Shore and Alan Young to play the leads. And they got us both—but good.

With Dinah Shore.

It was Dinah's first picture in years, and it turned out to be her last. As my rival for Dinah's affections in the movie, they cast Robert Merrill, that great voice of the Metropolitan Opera.

To top off the whole ridiculous caprice, the writer agreed to do the screenplay if he could direct it. He had never directed anything, but he wanted to try. The producers agreed.

After the picture was completed, I was asked to accompany it to a preview in Indianapolis. It was opening on the same night as the Indiana State basketball championship game! A bad omen.

Our press agent Bob Kaufman arranged an antique-car parade through the streets to the theater, with me out front playing the bagpipes. Behind the cars were Boy Scouts, each carrying an American flag. Bob didn't miss a bet.

Inside the theater were four rows of people, all Paramount distributors. They had to be there. During the opening scene, you could hear a pin drop. Which was a shame, because it was our best comedy spot. From then on it went downhill.

Back at the hotel I faced Bob squarely. "Level with me," I said. "Don't break it gently. How was it?"

"It's a flop," he said.

"Can't you break it gently?" I screamed. "Who's going to get the blame for this?"

"You are," he said, breaking it to me gently.

The phone rang. It was poor Dinah in Hollywood. "Alan deah, how was it?" she drawled.

"Dinah, I'm not going to break it to you gently. The picture is a flop."

There was the proverbial pregnant pause. I could picture those beautiful eyes of hers opening wide.

"Oh, how awful. Tell me, Alan—who is going to get the blame for this?"

"I'll break it to you gently, Dinah," I said. "You are."

I waited around and waited around. But, for some reason, my next big-money movie for Paramount was a long time coming. Again, I wasn't too upset. I had just signed with Howard Hughes and his recently purchased RKO Studio.

Hughes had just made a deal with the European producer Gabriel Pascal to film the George Bernard Shaw classic, *Androcles and the Lion.*

Because he was a television buff, the eccentric billionaire had seen my comedy sketches and decided he wanted me to play Androcles. One day I received a telephone call. "Mr. Hughes wishes to speak to you. He'll meet you on the corner of Gower and Melrose. Please be there at ten o'clock."

Very apprehensive, I was there on time. A dusty Chevrolet pulled up, the passenger door was flung open, and Howard Hughes beckoned me in. "I want to talk to you about Androcles," he said. "Please roll up your window."

It was a hot day, but I had heard about Mr. Hughes's peculiarities about eavesdroppers, so I obeyed. He started driving. It was some time before he said anything.

Even then, he spoke very quietly and kept his eyes straight ahead on the road. I could tell it was intended as a confidential conversation, because even I couldn't hear it!

I hated to keep repeating, "I beg your pardon?" all the time, so

I finally just nodded seriously and said "uh-huh" a lot. Finally he pulled over to the curb. "That's about it," he said and reached over and opened my door. "Good luck with *Androcles!*"

I got out and he drove away. I was now standing on the corner of Pico Boulevard and Sepulveda, a good five miles from where he picked me up. No buses or taxis, and the nearest phone booth four blocks away.

I got home at three in the afternoon in time to answer the phone call from my agent. "I hear you had a meeting with Hughes!" he said in awe. "What did he talk about?"

"Sorry," I said. "It was a tightly closed meeting. I couldn't repeat a word."

If Hughes's idiosyncrasies seemed bizarre, they were matched by the eccentricities of our producer, Gabriel Pascal. Hughes didn't want to hire Gabby, but he had no choice. Pascal had complete rights to film any and all of George Bernard Shaw's works. He was irreplaceable.

Many theories have been proposed as to how Gabby obtained Shaw's plays. He gave it to me firsthand. It all began one morning in London, when he was flat broke and at his lowest ebb.

He decided to skip breakfast and use the money to buy a train ticket to Ayot–St. Lawrence, Shaw's home in Hertfordshire.

At that time, Gabby wasn't aware that Sam Goldwyn, one of Hollywood's wealthiest and most successful producers, was with Shaw, trying for the same thing: film rights to all of Shaw's works.

"I will make your plays into cinematic masterpieces," said the producer. "I don't care if I lose a fortune as long as the pictures are artistic triumphs."

Shaw squinted at him. "I, on the other hand, don't care about artistic triumphs. I want to make money."

The film mogul left empty-handed.

Moments later, in walked a plump, disheveled little Hungarian with a gift of gab that Shaw spotted and liked immediately.

In his inimitable way, Gabby told the world-famous playwright the plays he liked, those he didn't, those which could make money, those which would be artistic triumphs and box-office flops. He concluded by saying, "I want to buy the rights to all your plays."

"How much do you have?" Shaw asked.

Gabriel took a shilling out of his pocket and smiled. "This is it."

"Sold," said Shaw, visibly delighted at Gabby's effrontery.

The deal was made and Gabby started for the door. Then he stopped and turned. "I haven't got the fare to London," he said. "May I borrow back that shilling?"

At first Pascal enjoyed great success with Shaw's works. *Arms and the Man, Major Barbara,* and *Pygmalion,* all produced in England, were artistic and financial successes. But somehow Pascal had frittered away the profits and was now at the bottom of his money barrel. *Androcles* was to be his comeback.

The cast for *Androcles* was impressive. Jean Simmons, the most beautiful face in any world, was Lavinia, supported ably by stalwarts like Victor Mature, Maurice Evans, Robert Newton, Elsa Lanchester, Jim Backus, Noel Williams, Gene Lockhart, John Hoyt, and Reginald Gardiner.

Incidentally, my costar the lion, was played superbly by actor-stuntman Woody Strode in a realistic lion-skin costume.

I was particularly thrilled to be working with that fabulous English actor Robert Newton, who was making his screen comeback after a tough, losing battle with booze.

Gabby asked me to keep an eye on Robert, who was playing the key role as Ferrovius. He wanted the actor to stay sober at least until the end of the picture.

So, on the first day of Newton's shooting, I was delighted to see Robert walk on the soundstage with a huge bag of oranges. "May I keep these in your trailer, Angus, old boy?" he asked, his head cocked and those black eyes boring out from shaggy brows. "My dressing room's outside in the sun, and there's nothing worse than hot oranges."

I assured him I'd guard them with my life. By noon, he had eaten every orange. After lunch, he brought another bagful into my room.

On the second day, the director came to me, looking concerned. "I must be wrong, but I could swear that Bob Newton is smashed! We've searched everywhere and can't find any bottles."

His suspicions were confirmed the next day, when Bob came to me just before a massive scene involving a few hundred extras.

"Angus, this is the parade of the prisoners into Rome," he said. "Wouldn't it be a delightful touch if, as we walked together, Ferrovius had his arm around little Androcles' shoulder?"

I agreed. Later Pascal and others remarked on the touching picture of the savage giant and the gentle tailor holding each other in brotherly embrace.

What nobody realized was that if I had let loose, Bob would have fallen flat on his ass. He was bombed!

To make matters worse, the summer sun turned our non-air-conditioned soundstage into a sauna. Bob was wearing padded robes and boots to make him look more mountainous. When he perspired, he smelled like a Siberian cocktail lounge.

"Cling fast to me, Androcles," Bob hissed, his breath almost knocking me unconscious. "The scene is progressing triumphantly."

I clung fast to him. Not because of the scene or the picture, but because he was one of the gentlemen of our profession, an actor with talents and frustrations that were pummeling him to death.

The next day, I discovered Bob's secret. I had left home without breakfast, so I decided to steal an orange from Bob's bag. I shoved a thumbnail under the skin, and juice gushed over my hand. I licked it off and cauterized my mouth. The "juice" was one hundred proof!

Bob had been systematically siphoning the juice out of the oranges and, with the aid of a hypodermic syringe, refilling the fruit with straight vodka!

In the opening shot of the picture, Androcles is sitting in his tailor shop with his wife, played by Elsa Lanchester.

In the room with them are various animals Androcles has befriended. There was a goat with one horn, a cat with a patch over its eye, a duck with a wooden leg, a three-legged dog, and a big black crow.

When the director shouted "Action," the cat was supposed to ride the goat over to me, the duck was to waddle under my chair, the dog was to sit up, and the crow would then fly onto my shoulder.

The bird's flight was the cue for the camera to pull back and include a window with people walking past outside. Then a group of centurions, led by Jim Backus, was to run up to the door, burst in, and arrest Androcles. It was an extremely ambitious "one-shot."

We prepared for one last rehearsal. The animals were perfect. They surrounded Androcles like loving children. Then, to everyone's surprise, a little butterfly fluttered down from the rafters above.

It circled the set, with the animals' heads rotating in fascination, following its meandering. Finally it fluttered out of sight. The crow then flew onto my shoulder, just as scripted.

The crew and cast burst into applause and laughter. Our unexpected winged visitor had relieved the tension. Now we were ready for the first take.

We were ready to go for it. "Action!" shouted the director and the scene began. Everything was going perfectly. I could hardly believe it. We were going to get the shot on the first take!

Then it happened. Just as the crow was crouching to take flight and finish a perfect scene, a voice broke out from the back of the set. It was Gabby. "Cut!" he shouted. "Cut!"

The set froze. Chester Erskine, our director, was so shocked that he couldn't move. Gabby walked center stage, turned to Chester, and asked, "Vere iss the butterfly?"

Two men restrained Erskine while another hustled Pascal off the set. When poor Chester finally cooled down, we began the scene again, but it took us all afternoon to get it right. Until the end of the picture, Pascal was barred from entering his own set.

       ✼   ✼   ✼

He said he had a hat.

"Androcles and the Lion" was released as a delightful, light Shaw comedy. And, with the release, Howard Hughes sold RKO—only to take the studio back six weeks later, when the buyers reneged on the final payment.

Hughes proceeded to withdraw *Androcles* from its limited release and ordered six weeks reshooting. To spice up the film, he wanted more scantily clad vestal virgins, more hand-to-hand combat action . . . and a real lion!

Apparently, he wasn't impressed by stuntman Woody Strode's impersonation and insisted on the real thing. Real me, real lion! At first I tried pleading congenital cowardice. But Hughes had seen my wild-animal act on television and insisted, "Young can handle the cat."

The first day of retakes, I felt faint when I discovered that a heavy chain-link fence encircled the set as they led in a huge, slavering beast. Mel Koontz, the lion trainer, shook my hand warmly and reassured me, "Don't worry. Jackie the lion is as gentle as a kitten."

I couldn't help noticing that Mel's hand was missing two fingers. A scar ran from his thumb to his chin. But he was a nice man, so I figured, "What the hell?"

The first shot opened with me beside a large boulder with Jackie crouching on the other side, about three feet away. I was supposed to crawl stealthily around the boulder and come face to face with the lion, then "cut"—a beautiful shot.

"Action," the director shouted and the scene began. All I could hear was the soft roll of the camera. What I could smell was another story: the breath of a live lion.

I couldn't see what was going on on the other side of the boulder. But apparently Jackie was acting up—getting ready to take a mighty swipe at me, I learned later. All hell broke loose when Mel the trainer appeared from nowhere, wielding a two-by-four plank which he broke over the uncooperative beast's head.

Jackie took off with a roar. His trainer kept after him, whacking the animal across the rump with the broken board.

"Don't get him mad, Mel," I screamed. "I've got to finish the scene with him!"

Jackie seemed to learn his lesson. He didn't get funny with me again until the final scene in the movie—and blood was drawn!

It was the dramatic, climactic moment where Androcles is kneeling alone in the vast expanse of the arena. The lion was to walk around me in ever-tightening circles.

The director called "Action!" I bowed my head preparing for the worst. And I almost got it as Jackie was goosed into action by Mel with a broom handle.

The tender scene in the film shows Jackie gently placing his paw on my shoulder. That's not exactly all that happened.

All I can remember is that godawful breath and his head landing in my lap. The next feeling I was aware of was his warm, strong jaws encompassing my groin. The pressure was gentle, almost loving.

I'm having a T-Bone well-done. He'd like the chef rare.

I realized that the animal wasn't attracted to me physically, nor did he want to hurt me. It was more like teething. He was young and afraid. I was older and petrified.

I could hear the camera grinding nearby. As we were filming without sound, any vocal expression was permissible as long as lip movement wasn't visible to the camera. "He's got me," I stage-whispered.

"Just a few more feet," somebody called, from his safe, comfortable vantage point behind the steel fence.

I attempted a surreptitious move. The frightened lion tightened his grip. He wanted to hold onto what he had. I wanted to save what I had. Maybe it wasn't much, but it was mine.

"Bite!" I screamed.

"The word is 'cut,' " the director replied in a loud, angry whisper. "And I'm the one who says it."

"The word is 'bite,' " I responded. "And I'm the one who just had it!"

Mel Koontz rushed in and gently removed Jackie's jaws from my crotch. I received a tetanus shot, a gentle, impersonal swab from the studio nurse, and that was that.

The scar can be seen to this day but I show it only to close friends or deserving charities.

A few weeks later I received a call from my press agent. "The preview of *Androcles* will take place next week," he said, "and I've got a great idea. You take the lion as your date!"

A coward would have hung up. A smart man would have fired him. But an actor says, "What time should I be there?"

I couldn't take the lion to the premiere, but he was quite acceptable for a TV interview at Ciro's afterwards.

The evening got off to an inauspicious start when Jackie relieved himself in the backseat of my car. Undaunted, I entered Ciro's with my date on a chain.

Upstairs, Jackie sat at a table and was as meek as a lamb while I answered reporters' questions. But when it was time to leave, the lamb reverted to lion.

Jackie was nervous about going down a steep flight of stairs, so he let out a loud roar, which was his way of saying, "Hey, I'm scared."

But to Herman Hover, Ciro's owner, it meant, "Enough's enough!" The Sheriff's Department was called, and Norman Greer, my imaginative press agent, saw a promotional dream come true.

In a banquet room on the floor below, United Press writers were having a dinner party. Norman ran in and interrupted their festivities. "Alan Young is upstairs with a berserk lion," he mentioned casually. "The Sheriff's Department has been called."

"Isn't Alan Young your client?" a sharp reporter asked.

"Yes," Norman replied, "but I wouldn't take advantage of that. There's a terrible thing going on up there."

The reporters began laughing and were waving Norman out of the room when suddenly Jackie let loose another deafening roar. They cleared the room in ten seconds.

Back upstairs, trainer Mel had a raw rump roast in his hand, trying to persuade Jackie to descend, while I was delegated to pushing the beast's rear end.

The newspaper contingent came rushing upstairs, cameras at the ready. With an entrepreneur's eye for promotion, Herman saw a golden photo opportunity. He dashed over and took a quick stance by the lion's side as the flashbulbs exploded. Then Herman headed for the fire escape.

The following morning, front-page news photos showed the brave owner of Ciro's directing the removal of a rampaging lion from his premises, as an unnamed actor is seen peering over the animal's behind.

By the way, we did manage to get Jackie down these stairs and into a cage without mishap. A year later, I was told that Mel had been almost torn to shreds by the same "gentle Jackie" who had bitten my crotch so lovingly!

A few months after that unforgettable premiere, the picture was released for a second time with a new promotional blitz. This time it was advertised as a gory, sexy adventure.

The public was somewhat confused. Was this another *Androcles*—a sequel, perhaps? RKO promoters were touting it as a *Quo Vadis, Ben Hur,* and *Demetrius and the Gladiators* rolled into one. "Barbaric revelry to fire the senses of the world," screamed the publicity blurbs. "The story of history's most sin-swept era!"

The gentle picture could not live up to this exaggeration. *Androcles* had a confused and mediocre run. Throughout the years, however, appreciation of the movie has grown and its new reputation is that of a film classic.

In the 1950s, one bomb and one mediocre movie were enough to shift a career into second gear. I had slipped into low and wasn't aware of it. Meanwhile, television had been taken over by westerns and giveaway game shows.

For the first time in almost twenty years, I didn't have my own show or a studio contract. I joined that coterie of artistic scavengers

At Ciro's Night Club with Herman Hover (owner), Paul Coats (*L.A. News-Mirror*), and Jackie.

who work from day to day, or week to week, as the guest spots present themselves.

Job security is unknown in the entertainment business. A television performer's job is up for grabs every few weeks. Contract-option time can have you celebrating renewal or registering for unemployment. But each day brings promise of that one big strike, the mother lode—a hit!

In 1990 the Screen Actors Guild reported a membership of 73,000, having more than doubled over the past ten years. Some 60 percent of this membership earned less than $1,000 a year! Only 12.1 percent earned over $10,000 per year, and of that percentage, only 3 percent were in the so-called big money of $50,000 a year or more.

The $25,000-a-year bank employee thumbs through his *TV Guide* and, with twinges of envy, reads about an actor getting thousands for one guest appearance. Don't twinge, friend, just smile and lean back. About 50 percent of the named salary is an actor's or publicist's exaggeration. This is the way he tries to keep his asking price at top dollar.

At the present time the average pay for the guest on a one-hour show is $2,500. For a half-hour, it's $1,500. And how many of these guest spots can an actor get in a year? The most popular actor is fortunate if he can get ten. So, at best, he's being paid the same money per year as the bank employee.

The only difference is that the actor's salary will be lessened by 10 percent to his agent, at least 15 percent to a manager. Then another 3 to 5 percent goes for accounting, advertising himself in trade and casting magazines, publicity agents, and union dues!

However, even with the guaranteed uncertainty of the acting profession, I know of no performer who would trade his precarious position for a job offering a predictable future. Oh, he might want to, but he's hooked. He's a theatrical junkie. There's a monkey on his back, and it's reading *Variety.*

History reports that in the 1850s cowboys began taking over the West. Whether or not this is true I don't know, but I'm witness to the fact that in the 1950s they certainly took over television.

Of the twenty top shows, eleven were westerns, with seven of these in the top ten! It took no psychic to predict that my career was in the toilet and somebody's hand was on the plunger.

Talk about rejection—at that point in my career, I'd been turned down more often than a motel bed.

That's the way it was in the 1950s. One flop picture, and they scraped the studio pass off your windshield!

Today if a performer hits a slump, he can hold a press conference and talk about how he overcame drug or alcohol dependency. Or he can pour out his soul in a best-selling book blaming parental abuse for all the ups and downs in his life.

In other words, if you stop doing something stupid, you can make a hero out of yourself. Or you can gain public sympathy by blaming your failure on a rotten childhood.

In my case, I lacked these opportunities. I didn't drink, smoke, use drugs, and my parents were very kind and loving. Gawd, if they only knew how much they hurt my career!

Today there are very few confessions inviolate when it comes to saving a sagging career. You can elbow your way into the public spotlight by revealing details about your sex life, be it good, bad, or peculiar.

But never ever let it be known you wear a hairpiece. Some things must be sacred.

But I digress. The final straw for me came early in 1956. My agent, Mickey Rockford of MCA, called. Mercury Motors was looking for a comedy show. Would I bring some films of my show over immediately? I picked out a couple of the best and rushed over to the agency office in Beverly Hills.

We played them for the agency men, and they howled their appreciation.

The agency loved the show. The sponsor loved it. What could go wrong? I found out the following morning.

Mickey had been in the business too long to break news lightly. "There was an end run," he said. "While we were viewing your show out here, the president of the company in New York bought Steve Allen. We haven't got a show."

Steve's show was an immediate hit, and it should have been. It was terrific. I couldn't be jealous, I was laughing too much. Later in the year, big-hearted Steve hired me for three or four guest spots.

Errol Flynn was a guest on one of Steve's shows and, being British colonials, we hit it off rather well. At the cast party afterwards, we sat together and I noticed he had just a glass of water in front of him.

He would smile pleasantly at me, take a sip, and converse happily

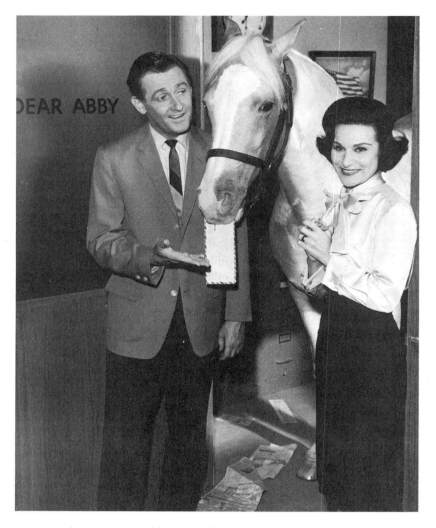

"I wrote a letter to Dear Abby cause she's got real people sense. She was so cute
I forgot what my problem was."

about cricket, a love we shared. We had another thing in common. Neither of us had any definite work to look forward to in the near future.

I couldn't resist saying, "Errol, you've been at the top and had everything you desired. Now, here you are doing a TV guest shot for comparatively little money, surrounded by people who are more successful, but not nearly as famous as you. How can you sit here tonight calmly sipping water and looking so pleasant?

He laughed. "Easy, old boy. I know tonight is going to end. Tomorrow is another day, and my agent will get me another job. And this isn't water. It's vodka."

He took another sip and continued, "The only way to exist in this stupid business is to stay pissed!"

The day after that Steve Allen show, I bumped into Eddie Pola, who had directed my ABC radio show. He was now the program director for Granada, a television company based in London. Eddie asked if I'd like to do a series for Granada.

Mulling over the pros and cons for at least three seconds, I agreed. I was going home.

On April 10, 1957, I stood at the rail of the SS *United States* watching North America sink into the horizon. Thirty years earlier, I had arrived aboard a leaky old freighter. Now I was steaming home on a luxury liner.

We were to broadcast our series from a converted music hall. London's Hackney Empire, a delightful old theater with gaslights still operating in the hallways and bathrooms. However, at that time, there was little joy in the experience.

We had just finished rehearsing the opening sketch when the director, an RAF type with a huge undulating mustache, bounded up to me.

"I say, old boy," he began. Then he laughed uncontrollably. "The most ridiculous thing's happened. You really—(stifled mirth)—really won't believe it!"

Our show was to be broadcast in a few hours, and we had rehearsed only one sketch. I had little time for giggling. "It sounds hilarious so far, but could you have the next set put up, and then we can have our laugh?"

"But that's just the point, old boy," he said. "The rest of the sets are outside. We can't get them through the door!

"And even if we could get them in"—he paused for more spluttering mirth—"even if we could . . . the sets were built to fit the Wood Green Empire. This is the Hackney Empire. They got the names mixed, don't you see?"

"I see," I said. "What I don't see is how we can get a show on the air tonight. We have forty-five minutes to fill, and only four hours until airtime. Any ideas?"

"Oh, not to worry," he said happily. "I thought you might fill in the time with some of your funny patter!"

Forty-five minutes of "funny patter"? I didn't have time to choke him, so I gathered the cast together for a desperate production meeting. We assessed the various performers' talents.

One of the propmen, I discovered, could play two tin whistles in harmony by shoving them up his nostrils and exhaling. He had a bit of a head cold so his act could turn disgusting from time to time. But the cameras were instructed to cut away when it became too obvious.

Two of the male dancers sang a medley of pub songs, accompanying themselves with rhythmic sounds made by flexing and pumping various parts of their anatomies—under the armpits, behind each other's knees, and so on. They weren't too good. But any port in a storm.

My contribution was an act where I played a bagpipe solo while one of the dancers did a striptease behind me. I would be unaware of the girl's presence and think the audience's reaction was for me and the bagpipe.

She would toss aside articles of clothing, and the audience would yell and applaud. Delightedly, I would ask the audience, "I'll bet you'd like another chorus!" or "Isn't this a pretty piece?"

In the movies, a story like this would end with the production being a big hit with rave reviews. But this was real life and London.

"Wilbur, I told you pilgrims shouldn't double park."

The following day, the kindest reviewer wrote: "Thank God for the nose flautist. He saved the day!"

Despite this opening farce, the series became a success. But British television is quite different from American. They will seldom produce more than six shows at one time. Hit or not, the show goes off the air to "recoup."

I was rescued from the English unemployment line just in time when film producer George Pal asked me to play Woody, the romantic lead in the Metro-Goldwyn-Mayer picture, *Tom Thumb*.

The romantic lead in an MGM musical? What a windfall! Not quite.

George explained to me that MGM wanted to make this picture in England on a shoestring budget. So, naturally, the actors had to take a sizable cut in salary.

I didn't mind too much. My show was on hiatus, George Pal was one of the nicest, most talented men I'd ever worked for, and I loved the cast. One of our costars was Peter Sellers, who had not yet hit his stride as a megatalent, but was getting up steam.

The picture wrapped. And now it was decision time again. British impresario Jack Hylton wanted me to do three more months of television in London, and there didn't seem to be any employment for me in the United States.

The U.S. Department of Naturalization made up my mind for me when the embassy notified me that if a naturalized U.S. citizen returns to his country of origin and lives there for five years without returning to the United States he is liable to lose his citizenship.

That did it. I realized that as much as I loved Great Britain, I had become an American in heart as well as on paper. I suddenly missed the United States. I missed California and, oh, how I longed for sunshine!

My lovely home with its spacious grounds was still there. Little did I know there was a horse waiting for me!

PART 3

Looking Back

10

Back in the Saddle Again ...
and Again ... and Again

After years of sitting up nights in re-write sessions, meeting with sponsors and agents, doing pick-up jobs, traveling halfway round the world, I was now going to stay in my own home, maybe forever!

No writing concerns, no worries at option time. We had a hit! About a year into the Mister Ed series the government made M.C.A. dissolve their talent division and now I no longer had an agent to worry about.

Week-ends were mine to use as I pleased; play golf, tennis, sail, garden, swim, things I'd always wanted to do. For the first month I did them all! Then fatigue and common sense took over and I settled for gardening and tennis. Who cared? I was at home!

Most of our "Mister Ed" location shooting was done in Griffith Park, an oasis of green in central Los Angeles.

It was a convenient locale, relatively smog-free with good, clean air—and, most important it was generally quiet during the week. Ed loved those trips to the park.

On one show, Ed wanted to learn how to fly a kite, much to Wilbur's embarrassment. So off to Griffith Park we went.

The first shot of the day showed Ed loping along with the kite string in his mouth. His first run was perfect. It was a take. But Ed had other ideas. He wanted to run some more, despite the fact that the crew had already turned their attention to the setup for the next shot, without Ed. To while away the time, dear Edna Skinner asked Lester the trainer if she could ride Ed for a bit. There must have been something reassuring about Edna that prompted Lester to say yes.

Edna mounted Ed and, as they took off, we all watched open-mouthed. Edna was racing Ed down the trail at an impressive full gallop, her long hair and his long tail flowing behind them in the wind.

It was a breathtaking sight. You could tell Ed was loving it. There's nothing more inspiring than a good horsewoman galloping at full speed and in complete control.

My admiration for her was clouded by twinges of guilt. I felt humbled when I assessed my own mediocre skills as a horseman.

A neophyte equestrian, what right had I to even pretend to put a magnificent five-gaited horse like Ed through his paces? As I watched Edna giving our star a decent workout, I couldn't help thinking, "Poor Ed . . . how does he put up with me?"

Shamed by Edna's example, I decided there and then to turn a new leaf, to become the best cowboy that I could be. I would take proper riding lessons.

Earlier I had made a halfhearted attempt at learning to ride properly. After the first half-dozen shows, I approached our wrangler, Lester Hinton, the man behind the horse. "Lester, it's occurred to me that I should learn to ride a horse properly."

"Occurred to me a while ago," he replied.

I didn't answer. I can be laconic, too. As if to make up for his snide comment he added, "I'll teach you."

At eight o'clock the next morning, I arrived at his "spread" in blue jeans and riding boots. For an agonizing hour, Les put me

"Gimme a little kiss, baby. No, not you lady—your horse!"

through the initial paces. That evening I was in more agony. Not only was my whole body stiff, but the flesh on my buttocks and inside leg was scraped raw.

The next morning I limped into Lester's barn and bleated out my tragic condition. "Oh, yep," he said. "That's what happens. You shoulda wore long johns."

"You didn't tell me," I whined.

"You didn't ask."

That made sense. I guess that was Les's way of making sure it was a valuable lesson I would never forget. Believe me, I won't. To this day I even wear long johns to sit on a bar stool.

Governing a horse on the set is a constant, energy-consuming occupation, so every trainer hires a wrangler to take over the more menial jobs such as currying, combing, and cleaning up.

In Les's case, he had an ancient cowboy with a real good-ole-boy name: Hank Potts. He *looked* as if he should be named Hank

"I finally get him to face the camera, and he closes his eyes. Jeeze."

Potts. He stood about five nine, weather-beaten face, tiny round nose, slightly crossed eyes, and a crooked, constant happy grin.

Over the years his legs had been broken, bent, and shattered. His knees had been operated on so much that they didn't bother with stitches, they just installed zippers. His poor legs were now so bowed that, like the old joke, when he sat around the fireplace he sat *around* the fireplace!

Topping off the whole picture was his stomach, which hung large and proud, completely obliterating his belt buckle, and attested to a lifetime of caloric contempt.

Lester thought the world of Hank, as we all did; so when Hank didn't show up for work one day, it caused great concern. Later in the day, a worried Les informed me that Hank had awakened in great pain, and his wife had rushed him off to the hospital. He was going through a series of tests, and they would probably know what was wrong in the morning. I had never seen Les so worried. He was even quieter than usual.

The next day Hank showed up with Les. He looked as fit as ever. When the people on the set asked him what had been wrong, Hank just shrugged it off and went to work. But I noticed a knowing grin pass between him and Lester. I didn't ask because I knew that Les would tell me in his own good time.

By mid-afternoon, I couldn't wait any longer. "Come on, Les," I begged. "What was wrong with Hank?"

Les grinned. "Take a good look at Hank. See anything different?"

I studied him. Same stomach, same legs, same pixie grin. And then I noticed. "He's wearing suspenders."

"That's it," Lester said. "He had terrible pains in his back, sides, and innards. They tested everything. Finally the doctors took a guess. They took off his belt and prescribed suspenders. Now he's fine."

Hank's gone now, but it wasn't until just a few months ago that I found out his history. It seems this gentle little wrangler who was so happy going about his business cleaning up Ed, mucking out the stable, and doing all the humble chores, had once been one of Hollywood's top trick riders and trainers.

"And he wasn't a meek little patsy either," Les said admiringly. "That bowlegged bastard could be real scary. I seen him."

It seems that in the 1930s Hank was head trainer in a western which starred a very egotistical macho actor. On the opening shot, the big star galloped up to the camera, and reined up in a showy slide. Hank suspected something. When the camera cut, he went up to the horse and examined the animal's mouth.

As he had thought, the star was using a spade bit. Effective and harmless in the hands of an expert, when it was used incorrectly, it was very painful and damaged the horse's tongue. Noticing blood around the animal's mouth, Hank removed the bit.

When the actor protested, Hank turned and stared at him, his cross-eyes blazing. He spoke quietly. "If I see you usin' this bit again, I'm gonna take it outa the horse's mouth and put it in yours. Then I'm gonna shove it up your ass. Better let me know your size."

But I digress. Back to the riding lessons which I had abandoned because of those painful early experiences.

I was overwhelmed with renewed enthusiasm after I saw Edna Skinner put Ed through his paces. Since Lester couldn't spare the time to resume teaching me, I asked him the name of the best riding master he knew. And that's how I met Red Burns, riding coach extraordinaire.

I knew Red wasn't terribly impressed with either my riding skills or celebrity status the first time we met beside the training ring at his riding school. He looked me square in the chest.

"You've bin doing the show for two years, and *now* you want to learn riding?" he barked. He had a way of making his introduction sound more like a dreadful accusation than a question.

Leaving the question hanging, he turned away from me to give gruff instructions to one of his pupils putting a steed through its paces in the ring.

"What the hell are you doing with that horse?" he bawled at the

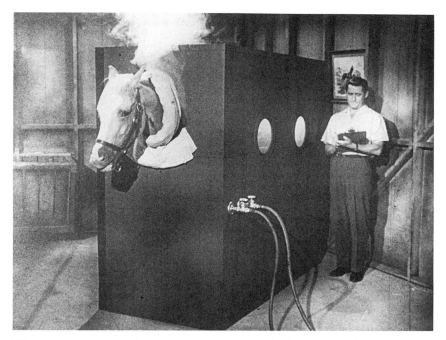

"She wants me svelte. Okay, I'll svelter. That's the kinda joke the other horses love down at the stables."

pupil. "After six months, you still don't know shit! You belong on a goddam bicycle!"

He swung back round to me, giving me his full attention again. "You want to learn to ride a horse? Or do you want to be a horse-man?" he demanded.

Already I had a choice to make and didn't understand the question. Naturally I guessed wrong. "I want to be a horseman," I said nobly.

Wrong answer, apparently. That's like saying you want to be a brain surgeon when all you want is to get rid of hiccups. I immediately knew I'd made a mistake. But stubbornness is one of my strong character traits, and the die had been cast.

The first thing I had to do was buy my own horse, never one of my most cherished ambitions. I ended up with a Morgan mare named Minx, who certainly lived up to her name.

The stable owner who sold me Minx assured me that she was extremely gentle with children. That sold her to me.

He neglected to tell me that she had no particular love for adults. Children let her do exactly what she wanted. The minute anyone out of puberty attempted to inject some of his own wishes and desires, she balked.

"She'll be good for you," Red tried to convince me. "Besides havin' to obey me, you'll have to make her obey you. That'll keep you busy!"

My lessons were four times a week, starting at 8:00 A.M. and they lasted for two hours. Before my first lesson, Red said, "I guarantee—in two months, you're gonna hate me."

I beat him by six weeks.

My routine was a constant: walk, trot, canter, gallop, stop, walk, trot, canter, gallop, stop, ad infinitum, ad nauseam.

However, Minx's routine was stand still, buck, kick, jump and, when desperate, lie down and roll over.

All of this was punctuated with Red's helpful and colorful comments, clearly audible as far away as Arizona.

The next exercise was doing figure eights in which the horse always took a shortcut, or tried doing two fours.

As my expertise improved—which means that I wasn't falling off nearly as often—the lessons became more complicated. At a full gallop, I had to pick a handkerchief off the fence rail. This I managed to pick up, along with a dozen slivers.

Another little bit of business I had to learn was to brake or rein suddenly, then remain seated topside while the horse slid for about ten feet—and all this at full gallop.

This I did. Then I outdid myself and slid another ten feet on my pants. And occasionally an additional five feet by way of an encore.

My tormentor, Red Burns, also instructed me to lean over with my right hand and touch the horse's stomach. Then do the same with the left hand while at full gallop again!

Minx didn't much like her stomach being touched. "Kiss me but don't touch my stomach" seemed to be her dictum, as she stopped suddenly and off I flew. I was grounded more often than an Iraqi pilot.

Finally, after what seemed to be an eternity, but what was really only an eon, Red conceded that I had made some progress. "At last you're governing your leather," he said.

"What is that?" I asked, reveling in the first encouragement I had ever had from him.

"Governing your leather means you are sitting right, handling your reins right. Your knees are gripping the flap, and your feet are pumping the stirrup," he said to my amazement.

Bursting with pride and accomplishment, I replied, "I've been doing all that? I hadn't noticed."

"Course not. That's why I had you doing it over and over until it was second nature," Red said gruffly. "No matter what the horse does underneath, if you are governing your leather you can't fall off."

He was right. I hadn't hit the deck in weeks. However, now that my long and expensive period of tuition was over, one thing puzzled me.

"Red, now the lessons are over, can you answer me one thing?

"Every day, while I've been sweating over these lessons, I've watched people riding out there in the hills—people I know have never had a lesson in their life. And they seem to be doing all right. Why might that be?"

Red chawed a bit, then expectorated. Cowboys always chaw a little when they're going to expound words of wisdom. Sometimes they chaw and expound without expectorating, but that can be quite gross.

"You just see them leave," Red drawled slowly after a long, careful pause. "But I see how they come back. Or I see the horse come back in without them. Or I see them carried back in. Not a pretty sight."

At the time, I didn't know whether to believe Red or not. But the following year I had the opportunity to prove his words correct.

While vacationing in London, I was invited by a friend to take

"We had good times together
. . . if I let him win."

part in a hunt. He assured me that there would be no fox but simply a spoor—a hunt that involved only hounds, riders, and a scented bag dragged across the countryside.

We met at a stable near Richmond Hill, just outside London. As I said, there was no fox, just a few yowling dogs. Our assembly was led into action by an odd-looking fellow, wearing a tattered old red coat and brandishing a bugle, who called himself Master of the Hunt.

My well-meaning hosts put me on a polo pony with an English saddle, which is about the size of a postage stamp. I looked down and couldn't even see it. But—, boy—could I feel it!

Just as I mounted up, the clown with the bugle let out a blast. My horse evidently didn't care for music. He took off like an unguided missile.

The rest of the group charged alongside me, galloping furiously up a hill shrieking weird words like "Yoicks!" and "Tantivees!" which I guess must be traditional English hunting cries.

The bugler must have been an excellent rider, because every so often he managed to steady himself at full gallop, get the bugle to his mouth, and let out a monstrous blast.

Many horses like to slow down until the entire pack has passed them, then accelerate suddenly until they are in the lead. This was the way my little polo pony liked to operate.

No matter how much I urged him on, he hung back defiantly. My pony was dawdling at the rear of the group as the Master of the Hunt, whose name was George, galloped past me barking out an order. Because of the clipped Brit accents and cries all around me, all I could hear was "Blah de blah de blah . . . trees!"

I thought, "Ah, he wants us to stick close to the trees." Before we mounted, I had heard a snide remark about Yanks not knowing much about this sport, and I was determined to show them I could follow orders with the best of them.

So, whenever a tree came in sight I swung near it, much to the delight of my horse, which maliciously selected the lowest branch to race under, causing me to duck repeatedly or suffer grievous bodily harm.

Finally, one of my friends came alongside and warned me, "For God's sake, Alan, George told us to stay away from the trees. There are potholes near the trees, and besides, your horse is trying to get rid of you!"

Eventually I wised up. But that headstrong pony wasn't finished testing me. He was again lagging at the rear of their group, then suddenly decided to make a charge to the vanguard, toward a grassy hill on the horizon.

My enthusiastic steed flashed past the others and reached the top of the hill in a few moments. I strained to rein him up in an effort to catch my breath which I had left some fifty yards behind.

However, Mother Nature had other surprises in store. As we hit the crest of the hill, we flushed a herd of deer which had been grazing in the underbrush.

I had never known, nor frankly even considered, what a herd of deer do when flushed. Like ballet dancers, they leap straight up into the air in a sort of entrechat, then, landing, do a grand jeté and zip off.

Well, along with buglers, my horse didn't much care for dancers. When the deer sprang into action, my feisty pony was fit to be tied. He took off in all directions.

"Well, I'm off to the moon.
I'll bring back some Brie."

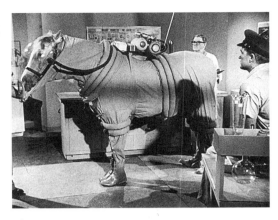

It was as if a Texas rodeo had been transplanted to the sedate English countryside. My pony bucked, braked, and galloped every which way but loose.

I was called upon to remember every little trick Red Burns ever taught me about staying on a horse's back. Although I say it myself, it was a superb performance of crisis management.

Glancing down, I saw my legs doing things I never thought possible. I slid professionally on the horse as it careered down hills and leaped over logs.

I touched his stomach and he touched mine. I could have picked up as many handkerchiefs, bottles, and old cans as I wanted to and never fallen off.

Oh, God! How I wanted to fall off. But my legs just wouldn't let me do it.

I reached the top of the next hill, the pace slowed, and it was easy to rein up my panting pony. In the lead, the Master of the Hunt turned and called out, "How many off?"

I looked back and, to my amazement, there were several empty horses cantering up the hill. I was one of the few survivors of what I learned later had turned out to be a hectic mass stampede.

The master looked at me with surprise mingled with puzzlement. "Jolly well done," he admitted reluctantly. "That was an interesting run."

I didn't tell him that would be my last one. I couldn't wait to return to America, get on dear old Ed's back, and just sit there in safety and comfort.

My days as a horseman were numbered. Let somebody else touch horses' bellies and pick up the stupid hankies!

11

Riding Off into the Sunset

I'll never forget the day old Ed and I rode off into the sunset.

All good things must come to an end. And, in the back of my mind, I guess I was always prepared for the day when Ed and Wilbur reached the end of the trail.

But I still wasn't prepared for the pangs of sorrow and nostalgia that overwhelmed me the day our cancellation was announced. A prop man came to me and asked, "You want any of Ed's stuff—his saddle, bridle, oat bucket?" He meant by way of mementos or souvenirs.

But I said no. I just wanted to leave.

The one bright note in those sad, final countdown days was that "Mister Ed" was riding into the sunset taking a huge audience rating with him.

In that respect, I think Ed was pleased to leave while the whole world still loved him. Better to have the audience ask, "Why on earth did you go off the air?" than "Why are you still on?"

The cancellation bombshell dropped one day while I was still in the director's chair—I hasten to state that these events were totally unrelated.

Our whole team was sitting around the conference table about to begin our usual read-over, a regular procedure which not only enabled the actors to get a feel for the story, but helped the producer, director, and writers ascertain what changes should or could be made.

Al Simon walked in and sat down. I had never seen his expression so serious. "Do you want to say something before we start reading, Al?" I asked tentatively.

He nodded slowly. "I'm afraid that when I've finished talking, there'll be no need to read," he said sadly. "We've done our last show. This script will never be seen."

For a few fleeting seconds, we thought that he was joking. But then, again, nobody jokes about things like that.

Still, the announcement was inconceivable to most of us. Our show was extremely popular, indestructible almost. It was the lead-in to CBS's complete control of Sunday-evening viewing: the unbeatable lineup of "Mister Ed," "Lassie," and Ed Sullivan.

Although "Mister Ed" came on the air a half-hour before what is known officially as "prime time" and had no regular ratings score, we did know that on a "sets in use" basis, our share of the viewing audience was around 47 percent.

In other words, taking into account the three networks and other local and independent stations, of all the television sets turned on in America, "Mister Ed" had 47 percent of that huge audience!

The only rational explanation for our axing was that CBS had a new program director, and he wanted to express his own ideas on scheduling. Changes had to be made, and we were among the casualties, regardless of our huge ratings and universal public acceptance.

Also, the new programmer might also have wanted to change the countrified—almost bucolic—image of the Filmways studio lineup.

Remember, as well as "Mister Ed," Filmways also introduced America to "Petticoat Junction," "Green Acres," and "The Beverly

"Arthur Lubin was our director."

Hillbillies." Now all but the Hillbillies had been cut, and "Mister Ed" was finally out to pasture.

Ed had had a great run. His theme song is probably as well known as "Home Sweet Home," and just as loved. The composers, Jay Livingston and Ray Evans who have written top-of-the-chart songs for over four decades, consider Ed's song one of their most popular. Ed won four Pasty awards. The award committee actually said to me just before the fifth awards that they had to give Ed second place, as it was beginning to look like a permanent situation. Ed didn't complain. He likes ribbons.

Few people realize that it was only from the profits and experience of "Mister Ed" that Filmways had been able to finance and produce the "Beverly Hillbillies" pilot, and other successive hit shows.

Like "Mister Ed," "Petticoat Junction" and "Green Acres" are still enjoying a long and healthy TV life in reruns.

Fortunately, it seems that you can never completely kill off a good thing, especially a show that earned itself such a special place in the hearts of the family viewing audience.

I'm sure that's the reason behind today's tremendous resurgence of the "Mister Ed" reruns, not just in the United States but all over the world. The show was originally translated into eight languages, so it now continues in 28 countries.

After the show closed, everyone wondered, "What about Ed? Is he going to be like every other actor who's lost a series? Does he now start taking 'calls' looking for another star vehicle? Or maybe he just ends up another out-of-work horse, seeking bit parts in westerns."

Loyal friends Arthur and Al took care of that. Out of the profits, they gave Lester Hilton a stipend that would take care of Ed for the rest of his life. Lester decided to retire and devote his time to caring for Ed.

Saying good-bye to Ed, Arthur, Al, and Les—the keystones of the show—was one of the saddest moments of my life. Success and money are all very well, but I'm sentimental. Relationships mean a lot to me.

I'd like to take time to say a few words by way of tribute to that loyal trio of Arthur Lubin, Al Simon, and Les Hilton.

As I mentioned earlier, Arthur's first great love and expertise was motion pictures. So, as a director, he approached every "Mister Ed" episode as if he was making a half-hour movie.

He never really fully understood or accepted the concept of television. Networks, sales, sponsorship, ratings, and all the paraphernalia of television were no part of Arthur's equation. That's not necessarily a bad attitude, but his genuine innocence proved almost disastrous in the beginning.

Before the show linked up with Studebaker as a sponsor, I had been without work for some time and was keen to see "Mister Ed" get off the ground. The go-ahead couldn't come fast enough for me.

There was an important meeting between our agents and the Studebaker people in South Bend, Indiana. It was supposed to be a simple signing on the dotted line, but two days passed, and I heard nothing. I was getting worried.

The bottom fell out of my world when our producer, Al Simon, phoned and said, "I'm sorry, Alan. I don't know what happened, but the whole deal is dead."

I later learned what happened at the meeting from my agent, Taft Schreiber of MCA. He was in the office of the president of Studebaker, who was surrounded by all his top executives.

The contract was in front of the president, who literally had his pen out and was about to sign when a door opened up and an aide asked him to step outside for a moment.

A couple of minutes later, the president returned. He picked his pen up, replaced it in his pocket, and said, "Gentlemen, we have no deal."

He threw a newspaper on the desk in front of them which explained every sorry detail. It seems that Arthur had celebrated the Studebaker deal prematurely.

Stopping over in New York en route to a cultural vacation in Rome, he gave an interview about the sale to a group of reporters. Dear, naïve Arthur couldn't resist exulting about the coup. After ten years of trying to interest somebody in his talking horse show, then making a pilot and having every network turn it down, it was finally bought by Studebaker, Arthur triumphantly bragged to reporters.

Naturally, buying a show that had been turned down so many times didn't appeal to the folks in Indiana. No way were they going to be treated like Hoosier hicks, bamboozled by slick Hollywood types. So we had no sale.

We finally got back on track again—but it took six months of planning, pleading, and reselling to put things right. By the time Arthur returned from Europe, everything was cool. And I doubt if he ever knew what happened.

In any case, a year later, Studebaker was out of business, though I was assured we had nothing to do with that sad occurrence. We now had a new sponsor, Post Cereal Company, and I was invited to lunch with the Post executive who had come from New York to oversee the new deal. MCA agent Mickey Rockford knew I was pretty good at the old ritual known as "romancing the client."

Arthur was free and, since he loved meeting new people and making new friends, he came with me. Mickey and the cereal mogul were waiting in a booth at the famed Brown Derby Restaurant when Arthur and I arrived. We sat down.

No sooner had the formal introductions been made, than Arthur said jovially to the Post VIP, "Well, I just want to tell you that I never start a morning off without a nice big bowl of Kellogg's Corn Flakes!"

We cringed—Arthur had done it again! Nothing was said. Post stayed with us. Maybe the guy thought Arthur was just kidding.

As a director, Arthur was indefatigable. He started the morning in high gear and kept pushing for the rest of the day. God help us if he wanted to get away early. He would burst into the make-up room around 7:30 A.M., saying, "Let's go. That's enough makeup. Forget the back of the neck—I'll never shoot it."

We would remind him that the Screen Actors Guild did not allow any filming until eight, and also that Abraham Lincoln had issued the Emancipation Proclamation in 1863. He would then hurry off, mumbling something about the Taft-Hartley Law.

Lest an impression be left that Arthur was not loved and respected, let me say here that it is almost thirty years later, and we have kept in constant touch.

He is a kind, thoughtful man who is totally without guile. He wouldn't like me to elaborate, but I know some of many generous things he has done for people and kept his deeds in the shadow of his own modesty.

The other bulwark of our show was Al Simon, another television legend and a true pioneer in the medium.

Al started out a successful newspaper writer, but show business appealed to his creative juices. He wrote radio shows, but when television came along, his innovative abilities found their niche.

Al produced "The Burns and Allen Show," which led him naturally to "Mister Ed."

"Why go to the Academy Awards? It's fixed, I never win."

When the Ed show was finally established and running smoothly, Al's creative juices began to flow in many other noteworthy directions. One day he gave me a script to read and asked for my opinion. I was flattered, although I knew he didn't want my advice but, rather, to share his new find with me.

It was called "The Beverly Hillbillies" and was a brilliant script. It became an instant hit for Al, and our show lost some great character actors when they became regulars on "Hillbillies." Raymond Bailey (our lawyer) became the Clampetts' banker, Donna Douglas became Elly May, and Frank Wilcox a supporting regular. However, since it was the same studio family, they would return to us now and again.

With "Mister Ed" and "Hillbillies" under his belt, Al spun off "Petticoat Junction" and "Green Acres." Then he produced "The Addams Family."

I can't think of any other producer who has had five hit shows on television at the same time! But Al is quick to say that "Mister Ed" was his first and greatest love.

Then there's Lester Hilton, a relatively unsung hero worth a book to himself.

I used to visit Lester's place on Sparks Street in Burbank, very near the Glendale park where we had shot so many of our shows. I was not alone. Each time I went to Les's place I found a few wranglers sitting around who had either worked with or knew our Ed.

If you have never met true Hollywood cowboys—or "wranglers," as they are called in the movie business—then you haven't met down-to-earth American originals.

Their laconic speech patterns make New Englanders sound like blabbermouths. "Yup" can mean either "You understand piss-all," or "Yes, up yours." And sometimes even "I agree with you."

Les didn't chew—or chaw—tobacco, but he always had a spittoon handy for his friends. Between thoughtful pauses, I would hear the resonant sound of a wad hitting the brass, which meant that one of the visiting wranglers had a statement to make.

"That Ed," our spitter would drawl. "Never saw a horse like him. He was special."

A lot of nods would follow, and then a long chewing pause. The spittoon would chime again, and all heads would turn expectantly toward the expectorator. " 'Member the time the script said he had to wear horseshoes with lifts to make him taller? Was that takin' a chance!"

Lester agreed, adding, "If Ed slipped I was gonna punch the director in the nose.

"Then there was the time they had him walk through the car wash to take a shower. He sure coulda slipped then."

"If he had, that director woulda got *another* punch in the nose."

Pause.

"Yup."

Enough talk for a while; now it was chewin' time. And time to

"I starred, did publicity, and pulled wagons. I worked like a horse."

reflect on all the adventures they'd had with that "good ole horse." All agreed they'd never seen a horse like that in their lives, and probably never would again.

Lester Hilton was a modest guy. The truth is, if there had been no Les, there would have been no Ed.

When a show flops, all are quick to disassociate themselves from it. Conversely, if it's a hit, they are just as fast to join the parade of individuals who want to claim an important role in the success. These are normal reactions, and the "Mister Ed" participants were no exception.

I've had my own fair share of hits and misses, but I must confess to a thrill of pride when Herb Browar, our associate producer, would say, "Alan, this show wouldn't have been a success without you."

Modestly, I would deny it, but deep down I thought, "You know, he may be right!"

However, the truth is—and we all knew it—the show could not have worked without the unsung, uncredited dedication and talent of Lester Hilton.

Les was the stereotypical laconic cowboy, only more so. Com-

"Director Wilbur is telling Larry what to do. Larry is about to tell Wilbur what to do. I hate scenes."

pared to him, Gary Cooper was a windbag. The usual response you got from Les was a nod or shake of the head, and even then he felt he was monopolizing the conversation.

The first week of shooting, I asked him, "Do you think the horse likes me?"

He didn't nod or respond, so I figured it was a stupid question. About the third show, Les looked at me and said, "Yep."

"Yep?" I asked.

"The horse likes you."

From then on, Les and I became very close. We didn't chat with one another, you understand. We just sat next to each other on the set and nodded a lot. One day he poked me and gestured for me to follow him. "Want t' show yuh somethin'," he said.

We walked into the stable where Ed was standing. Les lifted up the horse's muzzle and pressed one of Ed's nostrils open.

"Look in there," he said.

I had never looked up a horse's nose before, but I figured that since Les was finally trusting his friendship to me, the least I could do was stare at an open nostril. As an actor I've done all sorts of things that looked stupid, so staring up a horse's . . . well, I mean, it could have been worse, couldn't it?

"See the little blowhole halfway up?" he asked.

Sure enough, I saw it: a tiny hole about two inches into the nostril. It had a thin skin-covered valve that opened and closed with each breath.

"That's how the Indians would examine a horse," Les said. "It shows whether or not a horse has special breathing capacity. Not many people know that."

That was his message for the day. For the rest of the afternoon, we just sat and nodded. I was satisfied. I now knew something about horses' noses that only Geronimo and a few others were aware of.

Les loved the races. Nearly all of his spare time on the set was spent poring over the racing form, doping out every race. He knew the sire and dam of every horse west of the Nile, could identify their colors from an X ray, knew their successes on grass, dirt, mud, into the wind, with the wind, out of wind. What they did at Belmont Park, the Preakness, Epsom Downs, Longchamps, or other tracks. Les would have the race handicapped and off and running before you could say, "Who do you like?"

One day he pointed out all seven horses running that day at Hollywood Park. He quoted their history, lineage, earnings, every fact that racing literature had recorded.

That evening, I learned he hadn't been even close to picking a winner. I asked, "Les, with all that published information why did you lose?"

"Trouble is, horses cain't read," he said sadly.

If anyone could teach them how to read, it would have been Les. But, unlike any human athlete, statistics don't work with horses. They can be in perfect health, top shape, have an excellent jockey but as they near the gate it could be something they smell, see, or feel. Every statistic be damned—they just ain't gonna run.

As Les was telling me all this, I saw Ed looking at him with those huge, gentle eyes as if to say: "Gosh boss, if I could run you could count on me. I'd do anything you'd tell me."

And I'm sure Les knew that. It's why they were such good partners. If horses feel real love, I know Ed loved Les. I know Les loved him.

"Bath time!"

One of the big problems in a long-running series is choosing appropriate Christmas gifts. I like to make each one something personal, but after a year or two, it became a problem—especially with Lester. He didn't have much and he wanted less.

He didn't wear ties and already had a belt. I knew that if I gave him something fancy, he would pass it along to a friend or needy neighbor. On principle, I refused to give him a cigarette lighter, and his guests preferred spittoons to ashtrays. Then I hit on the perfect gift.

I was booked as a guest on Ronald Reagan's "Death Valley Days," playing the life of William Stetson, creator of the famous hats. In addition to my salary, they promised to have a couple of hats custom made for me, and further personalized by printing my name on the sweatband. I requested one for me and one for Lester, and they agreed.

When Lester opened the box, his mouth fell open. I'm sure I detected a tear of delight. He gave me a nod of thanks and spent the rest of the afternoon feeling the soft felt and reading his name.

The next day, I expected to see him decked out in all his new finery, but instead he was wearing his same old beat-up straw lid. It was the same for the rest of the week. Finally I asked him, "Why aren't you wearing the Stetson, Les? Don't you like it?

He looked at me in puzzled astonishment. "Aw, that hat is too good for me to wear. That's for hangin' up and lookin' at."

A few weeks after our wake for the show, I headed east to begin rehearsals for a Broadway play.

It was a full year before I returned to Los Angeles. One of my first stops was at Lester's place to visit my friends. Les had sold the old "spread" and had bought a tiny house on Sparks Street in Burbank, California, with a small backyard, paddock and barn. He decided that he and Ed would share the place for the rest of their days. Understandably, he would have the house and Ed the barn.

From then on, whenever I was in town, Sparks Street was my first stop. Les barely hid the fact that he was glad to see me and almost immediately told me "He's out back." Could Ed be anywhere else?

It was always a heart-jump to walk out to the back yard and see that handsome head poke over the barn's half-door to welcome me. The big brown eyes shining, the ears forward as if eagerly waiting for a cue. You can take the horse out of show business but, well, you know the rest. Lester would undoubtedly shake his head and say, "Funny, he was asleep until you got here."

One day I dropped in and Lester quietly asked me to sit down. When he didn't invite me out back, I knew.

A few weeks before, Lester had paid a quick visit to relatives in Oklahoma and he had a wrangler stay to take care of Ed for a few days. The man knew everything about Ed's habits and needs except one. No one is quite sure what happened exactly, but it would appear that Ed decided to lie down or perhaps take a roll in the

"Our makeup man, Jack Pierce, wore out three puffs powdering my nose."

grass, which was not his usual routine. He was a heavy-bodied horse with long slender legs, not always strong enough to get himself back on all fours without a lot of flailing and struggling.

The poor "sitter" came out to see Ed on the grass puffing and heaving and thought the horse was having some sort of seizure. He held Ed's head down to stop him from struggling. Ed was used to this from his training and lay quietly. The man then shoved a tranquilizing pill of some sort into his mouth.

It might have been the fact that Ed was not used to the medicine or some other reason Lester couldn't figure out, but, within hours, Ed was gone. He was cremated in Los Angeles, and where his ashes were scattered, only Lester knows.

For the first time, I saw Lester's emotions on the surface and it was like a father who had just lost his only son. Later he told me that though the reruns were on television every day, "I just can't watch them no more."

"I know the hat isn't me, but I'll eat the cherries later."

A few months later I visited Lester again, this time in the hospital, and within a matter of weeks, he too was gone.

Ten years ago, the newspapers carried an account of Mister Ed's death somewhere in the midwest. Then I read of the people in that area raising a fund to erect some sort of monument to his memory. Reporters called to ask my thoughts. When I heard that the folks had raised the money for Ed's burial and had already built the statue, I found it difficult to shatter their illusions. It seemed only fair to say that it was good of them to build a memorial, but I knew Ed wasn't under it.

The only possible explanation for this false report was that in 1960, before the show started, Filmways, the studio which filmed the series, shot some publicity stills, using a rented palomino. Later it was learned that after the show's success someone, possibly the one who rented Filmways the horse, was showing his animal around the country as the original Mister Ed.

At first the studio thought of taking action to stop this but felt it was innocuous and let it go. Evidently this was the horse that died in the midwest. In any case, I know my Ed isn't jealous about sharing the billing with someone else. Look what he did for me!

Eight years ago, Nick-at-Nite, a division of the Nickelodeon Cable Network bought the distribution rights for Mister Ed and began running the show again. It caught on immediately. After years of almost total obscurity, Mister Ed galloped across the screens of America.

The cry "Aw, Wilbur!" is again heard throughout twenty-eight countries in what must surely be one of the greatest comebacks in show business.

I have attended many memorabilia shows throughout the United States, where thousands of people come to see and meet the performers, view old shows and get autographs and pictures.

The stall is empty, the phone unanswered.

Three generations of Americans come to reminisce, relive and enjoy their beloved Mister Ed. As of this writing, I'm now being swamped with calls for interviews and appearances.

A question I'm often asked is, "I guess you get tired of talking about the horse after all these years, right?"

I answer honestly, "No way."

Today no matter what subject I'm being interviewed on, the questions turn invariably to Ed. I had felt that the passing of years might enable me to get rid of the horse, but that was not to be. He's on my back now, and I don't mind a bit!

Interviewers generally start with, "It must have been interesting working with a horse. Tell us a few of the funny things that happened." And there's nothing to tell. Ed handled his part with superb professionalism.

How can you tire of discussing the handsomest and greatest actor you ever worked with? An actor who was humble, always ready to please, asked for so little, and carried me on his back all the way.

A horse is a horse, of course, of course. But Ed was Ed. I'll never forget him.

12

Still Riding Along

After "Mister Ed" rode off into the sunset, I thought seriously about quitting show business. But I felt I needed a last hurrah—and what better stage for a swan song than Broadway!

Working New York's Great White Way is probably the most thrilling and satisfying adventure in the business—something that every performer hopes and dreams for. It's often been called "the impossible dream," and for good reason. There are probably about a thousand plays and shows submitted to agents every year. And only about ten ever reach the production stage.

After endless, tiring months of rehearsing, rewriting, and trying out in various test cities, perhaps three may reach Broadway. Then one flops, two stay, and one might be lucky to stay for a year.

Thousands of performers audition for Broadway-bound productions. Three hundred may be selected for further tryouts, and about 50 end up getting cast.

Then begins the grind of rehearsals and out-of-town tryouts at rehearsal scale, the lowest salary unions will allow. Sometimes a show will get only as far as Boston and close—or, if it gets to New York, close after one night.

Pity the poor actors! Six months out of their life away from home, and no money saved. Then it's unemployment time again. All they can do is read the trade papers to seek out yet another audition.

My big Broadway moment was as the star of a comedy called *The Girl in the Freudian Slip.* Since the production originated on the West Coast, we did our initial rehearsals in Los Angeles for six weeks, then had our debut performance in Phoenix.

After our first few performances, it was obvious we had a very funny play. But it still needed a lot of work.

There were rewrites after rewrites, until it got to the stage I didn't know whether I was coming or going. Scenes were rewritten completely. My dialogue changed from night to night.

There were times I stood helplessly onstage, my heart in my mouth, not terribly sure of where I was. Or what I was supposed to say!

I'd make an entrance, and start worrying: "Let's see, shouldn't I be over there? I could have sworn there was a table there last night. Where's Marjorie Lord? Oh, that's right—she's not due to enter for two more lines. Speaking of lines, what's mine? No, that's not it—that's been cut. The new line is . . . what? Is it too late for me to go back to Canada!?"

A stage can be a terribly lonely place at times like that. Your heart stops and starts countless times, and the flop sweat drenches your entire body.

Once we were convinced we had got it right, we moved to Broadway. When our show got there in March 1967, the newspapers were on strike. And there can be no shows without newspapers. So, for six weeks, the whole cast had to sweat it out in a hotel—and wait.

The strike over, we moved into the Booth Theater, in Shubert Alley, the heart of Broadway, to begin two weeks of previews— half-price shows so stagehands could get used to the backstage

"Gee, your hair smells terrific!"

equipment and actors could grow accustomed to their new surroundings.

We hadn't faced the critics yet, but word-of-mouth indicated we
had a hit on our hands. We played to sold-out preview houses,
amid laughter, applause, standing ovations.

The younger actors became convinced this was going to be their
big break—one of the newcomers on our show was Bernadette
Peters, the understudy for my stage daughter. Her dream was to
come true . . . but a few years later.

Previews over, the big night arrived. I felt comfortable with the
show now; but no matter how confident you are, when that big
opening night comes along, the butterflies still line up outside your
navel!

In the audience was a man who could make us or break us—
Walter Kerr of the *New York Times*, the dean of the Broadway
critics.

Kerr was getting ready to retire. He had just one more show to
review: ours. We had a couple of strikes against us: we were a
Hollywood show with Hollywood actors. And we were opening in
June—definitely not the best time of the year.

But the evening went off well. The first act was still a bit shaky,
but we picked up steam and came through with very strong second
and third acts. Anyway, the curtain went down to laughter, applause, and yet another standing ovation.

Confidently, the cast assembled in the famous Sardi's Restaurant
to await the critics' reviews in the morning papers. Dinner patrons
applauded and gave us another standing ovation as we walked in.

Trying to appear nonchalant, I thumbed through a newspaper
during my meal trying to find a suitable New York apartment to
rent—oh, say, for about a year. That's all the time I wanted to stay
with the show.

Suddenly the restaurant became quiet. The papers had arrived,
and people were scanning the reviews. What? Walter Kerr didn't
like it? How much? Are you saying he hated it?

Yes, he hated it—and the other critics endorsed Mr. Kerr.

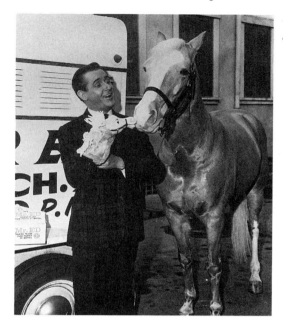

"A puppet's a puppet, of course! of course!"

I waited until the restaurant emptied and walked home by myself. It was two in the morning, and I remember walking close to buildings and under awnings so no one could see me.

I didn't want to take a taxi—because I knew cabbies liked to read the early editions, too. . . .

So, in the summer of 1968, I quit show business after having been in it from the age of thirteen. I had saved my money—not a lot, but enough to get by.

It wasn't a sudden decision. My bitter Broadway experience might have had something to do with it. But it was by no means the catalyst.

A few years earlier, in the middle of the "Mister Ed" series, I said to myself (the horse would never listen):

"Alan, you've had a good life since you came to America. You had your own radio show, made movies, wrote and starred in your own television show. What are you going to do when you finish this series?"

"Are you talking to me?" Ed asked suddenly.

"No, just thinking out loud." I said. And my mind was made up. I had always felt such gratitude for my faith and my adopted country, that I had long wanted to change to an occupation where I could spend 100 percent of my time sowing something back into this land.

Politics was out. A naturalized citizen could never be president, and a ham always has to try for the top. Also, I could never figure out the difference between Democrats and Republicans.

As a longtime student of Christian Science, I decided to work in the pure atmosphere of religion. Little did I know!

If I had studied the lives of independent religionists a little more, I would have seen that there's only one thing more brutal than throwing a Christian to the lions, and that's throwing a lion to the Christians.

It would be easy for me to launch into a sermon on spiritual values here, but suffice to say that after seven years of firsthand experience in church affairs, I became sadly disillusioned.

Maybe I was too idealistic when I became involved in the affairs of an organized church with such zeal. That's why my gradual realization that organized religion dwells so much on the acquisition of bureaucratic power and money, that the teachings of the Good Book tend to get overshadowed, made me feel very uncomfortable.

I don't mean to suggest evil intent here. It just turns out that way. Like a pregnant woman, bureaucracy is going to grow bigger no matter what. And religion's bureaucracy is no different.

In the eyes of the church hierarchy, I was an intruder, maybe even a threat. I guess I was rocking the boat and just wouldn't sit down.

Not that my efforts to help make a difference were ever taken seriously. I'll never forget when one of my church's respected members of the hierarchy said to me, "It's good to have you here with us in Boston, Alan. Every court needs its jester."

He did to me what no heckler in all of my show-business experience had ever done: he left me speechless. I realized that it wasn't his fault. He knew only what he had been raised with and was doing the best he could. I was the intruder.

If you really know you have done your best and have nothing else to offer, then don't overstay your welcome. And don't try to force your opinions and theories against overwhelming resistance. It's best to fold your tent quietly and take off.

So I took off. I had learned a lesson. That which I believed, I believe still. And I still try to practice and live those truths effectively and unobtrusively.

Now it was necessary for me to reenter "the business." I wasn't actually welcomed home like a prodigal son, inundated with all kinds of great job offers. It was more a case of "Back to the end of the line for you, fella!"

In the seven years I had been gone, television had changed and grown. Shows' budgets and stars' salaries had trebled and quadrupled.

Having an agent represent me was now vital, but try to find one! Who wants to spend time trying to sell a man who retired at the top of his career and turned his back on a fortune? Also, a false rumor had spread that I was a minister. I dampened a few parties by just showing up.

Dinner theater was in its prime in 1975, so I managed to pick up some bookings. It was good, not only for my bank account, but it helped me reestablish confidence and timing.

While other stars of my era were playing theaters in Chicago and Miami, I hit the barn theaters in Lubbock, Texas, and Albuquerque. But the audiences were great. I was back in show business and loving it! However, I still couldn't crack the Hollywood scene.

One day Gary Krisel, a young man who was in charge of the music recording division of Walt Disney Productions, called me.

He knew I had written for radio and asked whether I could write an album based on Charles Dickens's *Christmas Carol,* using all of the Disney characters.

My old pal Alan Dinehart, the television director, knew the car-

"This is Wilbur being made up to look like his father."

toon business inside out, so we teamed up, wrote the script, did the voices, and produced the album "Mickey's Christmas Carol."

It turned out to be a great seller. Disney decided to turn it into a motion picture, with me doing the voice of Scrooge McDuck.

This led to the Disney series "Duck Tales," the adventures of Scrooge McDuck and his nephews Huey, Dewey, and Louie. This turned out to be one of television's biggest animation hits. I had finally reentered show business through the voice-over door.

The voice-over industry is one of the tightest cliques in the business. But, having been raised in radio, it was like home to me. There's very little credit or recognition, but the money's lovely,

There is a whole world of talented people out there whose voices fill the homes of the world. But their names and faces are totally anonymous and unfamiliar.

Don't feel sorry for them. Their incomes are greater than most on-camera actors. And they never have to worry about getting fat, thin, old, or wrinkled.

With my foot in the door again, it wasn't long before I hooked up with a manager—Gene Yusem, who also acts as agent, publicist, and friend. I think my contract with him ran out some years ago, but it doesn't matter. I don't know where it is, anyway.

Gene has kept me busy with television series, guest-star roles, and theater.

The amazing and unexpected icing on my cake is the rebirth of "Mister Ed." It has been in syndication for many years, and the only concrete evidence I have of its longevity have been the profit-participation checks I receive at the end of each year.

A few years ago, the amount was so small that I was told it probably indicated the series' last gasp.

Then, suddenly, the nostalgia bug bit America. Whether audiences were fed up with the cookie-cutter production methods of today, or sated with the sameness of sitcoms, I don't know.

Nickelodeon Cable Network purchased "Mister Ed," along with many other old series, and that was the beginning. Today Ed is again galloping all over the world, and I am happily going along for the ride.

The continued popularity of the show is mind-boggling.

Two years ago, I stepped into a crowded elevator. The crazy thought came to me to do my own consumer test. As I faced the door, I quietly sang the first line of our theme: "A horse is a

"This is his father made up
to look like Wilbur! How 'bout
those sponges."

horse"—then stopped. In unison, my fellow passengers behind me finished with ". . . Of course, of course!"

And now I hear that the owners of "Mister Ed" have been asked to consider doing an Ed movie, or another TV series, or maybe a movie-of-the-week, thanks to the recent big-screen successes of old shows like "The Beverly Hillbillies," "Dennis the Menace," and "The Addams Family."

We are considering these ideas carefully. None of us is in a hurry to make a mistake. The memory of the show is too precious.

For me, "The years that the locust hath eaten have been restored"—and I'm still in the business I know and love best.

We keep on riding.